Everything Under The Rainbow

(Or At Least As Much As I Could Fit Into This Book)

Other Books By Oskar Leonard

Our Paused World
Twisted Bloodlines
Lighter Fluid

Everything Under The Rainbow

(Or At Least As Much As I Could Fit Into This Book)

By Oskar Leonard

oskarleonardofficial@gmail.com
https://oskarleonard.wordpress.com

This collection is dedicated to Scott, Karen, Toni and all of the other youth workers and volunteers who have helped with BYOU, as well as the members themselves. Thanks for being a supportive group and an entertaining, if chaotic, break from everyday life once a week.

Contents

Introduction

Hi there! Before you read this collection, I'd like to introduce it and explain a few of my thought processes behind creating and publishing it. I'd also like you to know that whatever your identity is, you are welcome here. Whether you're an LGBT+ young person looking for representation and help, an ally who wants to learn more or a parent trying to find out ways to support and understand your child, I'm glad you're reading this.

I'm a transgender and bisexual person, so I understand the struggle of trying to find good LGBT+ representation in media (although it is getting better!). I also know that it can be hard to find the resources and information you need when education is sometimes lacking and services aren't advertised well, or at all. This collection is my attempt to combat these issues and bring a little bit of fun and hope to your day.

You may have already skimmed through the book and noticed that I've put content warnings before each short story. This is something I haven't done before, but I felt it was especially important for these stories, as many cover potentially distressing topics. Reading through each list should give you the space to choose whether you read that story or not. As a side note, these stories are all in pre-Covid-19 settings—I think we all need a bit of a break from that particular aspect of life right now.

All in all, I hope this collection helps you—I know it would've helped me a few years ago. Feel free to read on and enjoy!

-Oskar Leonard.

Summer Solitude

Summer Solitude first appeared in Revolution Publication

Content Warnings

Social Anxiety
Mention Of Unsupportive Family
Mention Of Alcohol
Mention Of Underage Drinking

Charlie, they/them

Friendly conversation flittered around the corridor. Summer plans and holiday destinations and everything else you'd expect from the last week of high school before summer.

I really wanted to join in, you know. More than anything. But, instead, I found myself standing silently by the other students gathered around the door to Room 0010. I studied the rather boring, plain wall opposite me.

With summer approaching like an unstoppable, juddering freight train—like the one that rushed past the park in the middle of town—we waited for the last session of our school's LGBT+ group.

Mrs Linn would arrive soon. Then we'd all file in, still chatting and joking. Introductions, then discussions. Everything ran smoothly, unlike most lessons in our high school. There again, our group was far from being a lesson. We'd have a few minutes for reflection or meditation, whatever you wanted to call it—that was an addition suggested by one of the PSHE teachers. Then, we'd leave. Still chatting. Still joking. Off to the last lessons of the day, then home.

Home. Or the awkward quiet of an unsupportive house.

"Yeah, going on holiday this year. Dad swore he'd take us somewhere nice, like, but he said that last year."

"Where'd ya go last year?"

"Park down the road. Ay, is that Miss?"

Catching that last little snatch of conversation, I jolted my view away from the wall. Was she here? Looking up, I saw only the passing crowd of black-blazered kids drifting down the corridor in little friendship clumps. None of them looked at us. Their eyes stayed down, or on each other, their mouths constantly curved into half-smiles which anticipated corny jokes and cornier insults.

Was it because they knew it was an LGBT+ group? Or was it just teenagers being teenagers? It was so hard to tell. Straining my eyes, I glanced further down the corridor. Kids, kids, kids... wait. That soft-looking, light-brown hijab. Those chunky, cherry-red glasses. Could it be?

Did... did I want it to be Mrs Linn?

There was nothing I enjoyed more than the LGBT+ group's weekly meetings. Friday lunchtimes were blissful because of them. But this one was different. This one meant that everything was over. The safe space, the warm classroom, the friendly faces... they'd all be gone for six long, excruciating weeks of loneliness. Six weeks trapped at home with parents who didn't really know who I was. Six weeks to sit, and think, and wish I could be back at school.

Everyone would call me crazy if I told them that. Even among people like me, I still didn't really belong. I didn't talk. I didn't chat. I'd tried but getting a word in edgeways was more difficult than some exams. They were a chatty bunch, between ten and fifteen kids showing up on any given day. I could tell you all of their names, but I don't think they could tell you mine. I only whispered it during the introductions, and nobody paid attention anyway.

This was my support. My 'rock'. A group who I didn't really talk to or interact with. Sometimes, life just didn't make sense.

"Hey, guys! Everyone looking forward to summer?" Mrs Linn was full of the holiday spirit, which seemed to have completely bypassed me. "Is the door locked?"

"It always is, miss," someone replied.

"Just checking!" Bright and smiling as ever, she took a key from her staff lanyard (yellow; easy to notice, I suppose) and rattled it around in the door. It opened with the usual click.

Not unlike a herd of cattle, we were ushered into the room by the smiling teacher. Three Year 7s (their names blinked in and out of my memory, disappearing at that particular moment) surged forwards and threw around some chairs. Nothing to be alarmed by.

That was just their version of 'getting the room set up'.

I hovered by the door as everyone put their bags down, slouching into mostly cracked and graffitied plastic seats. As ever, I needed somewhere to sit. Also as ever, I had no idea where to sit. Somewhere between friendship groups, but not too close to anyone... I was putting way too much thought into this.

As ever.

Sighing quietly, I navigated around the minefield of chairs, coats and bags. Tables had been haphazardly shunted pretty much everywhere. It was a health and safety nightmare, but Mrs Linn didn't seem to mind. She was just nice like that.

The blinds were down, to give us some sort of 'privacy' or 'security' or something of the sort, despite the obvious posters plastered all over school saying 'LGBT+ Group - Join Now! - Room 0010 - Friday Lunchtimes!'. They were trying, I guess, but they could have done with putting a bit more thought into it.

You could tell they put some effort in, though. It was in the plain sheets of paper blue-tacked to the slim, rectangular window in the door, the kind of thing they put up for exams. Not much. Not revolutionary, by any stretch of the imagination, but it was something. I appreciated 'something'—I'd always rather have 'something' than 'nothing'.

"Alright, has anyone got a question for us?" Mrs Linn perched on the teacher's desk, left untouched by the Year 7s' antics, facing us all. We'd sat in a wobbly circle around her. Everything seemed like it should've been normal, but I knew it was different this time. "Anyone?"

She looked around expectantly. Everyone fell silent at her question, ironically asking for a question, because we all knew what came next. Blood began thumping past my ears. I held my hands together, my fingers gripping each other tightly.

Please don't call on me. Please don't call on me. Please don't call on me.

"Holidays," a voice grunted, the same voice which complained about their disappointing holiday with their dad on the corridor, "some'in about holidays."

"That'll do," she smiled back at them, nodding in that supportive, teacher-y way, "what are your plans for summer? Holidays, parties, seeing family, hanging out with your mates—oh, and please, folks, keep it PG. I don't want a repeat of the 'favourite drink' question."

A few people chuckled. My lips wavered a little, wondering whether to move, but my mind shut down that notion quickly.

It was funny, though: learning everyone's preferred alcoholic beverages as Mrs Linn's face got redder and redder with every new answer.

"Okay, who'd like to start?" No hands, no volunteers. No one liked going first. "Right, let's see —well, you came up with the question," she waved a hand at the person who was cheated out of a holiday by their dad, "so won't you start us off?"

They grunted in response.

"Alright, name, pronouns and your summer plans," Mrs Linn nodded warmly at them. They sat up and grinned back.

Everyone, secretly or not-so-secretly, liked Mrs Linn.

"   Nova, they/them, not much."

"Not much?" Mrs Linn asked, her head inclining a little.

"Might go on holiday," Nova finally said, crossing their arms and slouching once more. Their turn was over.

Now, I just had to wait until it was my go. Chilled sensations swirled around my stomach, with no regard for the sudden nausea they caused. I gulped. The introductions snaked around the group, getting closer and closer.

I gulped again. Twice. Then thrice. My throat remained dry.

Name, pronouns and holiday plans. Name, pronouns and holiday plans. I could do it. People were spitting them out at the speed of light, again and again. Too fast. I'd be next in a second—a millisecond.

It was always like this. I would never get used to it. Just like circle time—just like drama—it was something that made me speak in front of everyone else.

I hated speaking in front of everyone else.

"Alright, it's you next!" Mrs Linn chirped, looking straight at me. Wanting to melt into the floor, I hesitated before nodding. "So, name, pronouns and summer plans."

"I-I'm Charlie," I stuttered through the introduction, blinking fiercely to try and subdue the threatening tears which made my vision blurry, "I'm Charlie, I use neutral—uh, they/them pronouns, and my summer plans..." naturally, my mind blanked, leaving me with a few seconds of awkward silence, "uh, I don't know."

"This question doesn't work, no one knows what they're doing," someone cut in, "like, everyone's said nout."

"Ay, I said I was going on holiday!"

"Next person, please!" Mrs Linn interrupted the interruptions, waving a hand and demanding silence. The talking stopped. She wasn't a strict teacher, but she was the sort of teacher you didn't disobey out of respect. It'd feel like disappointing a friend.

The introductions moved on, then ended. My lungs filled themselves with warm, stuffy classroom air, not helped by the closed windows and door. A discussion began. But, busy recovering from being forced to say something (which shouldn't have been a shock, since it happened every week, but my brain always treated it as one) I didn't really participate. Or listen, much.

Until Nova mentioned summer.

"It's gone be difficult, innit? For some of us, I mean," they started, clearing their throat, "us with less good parents, like."

"Yes, yes," Mrs Linn said, drawing her mouth into a thin, serious line, "without school, and this group, summer might be difficult for some of you. But what can we do to try and facilitate that?"

Personally, I didn't really know what 'facilitate' meant. I'd heard of it, but I couldn't use it without being afraid of sounding like an idiot, or a posh so-

and-so. All I knew was that I'd abolish summer holidays in a heartbeat, and probably get hunted down and put on a stake for it.

Mrs Linn's idea, since she definitely already had one despite asking the group for our own ideas, was an online group. A group chat, Nova informed her, was what they were called. Something informal (read: non-teacher-related) but supportive. Helpful but casual.

It sounded perfect. Finally, a solution to the terrible summer I was anticipating—a little digital hideaway, where I could at least read about what everyone else was up to. Actually sending a message might've been a little beyond my capabilities.

But, as Nova travelled around the classroom, Mrs Linn deciding to ignore the blatant flouting of the school's 'no mobile phones ever, anywhere, don't even think about them' policy, I was passed by. Again, and again, and again. Sinking into my chair, I fixed my eyes on one particular spot on the blind-covered window, a little square of errant light which had squeezed its way into the room. Maybe I could squeeze through there and disappear outside if I stared hard enough.

It didn't happen. Predictably.

Time ticked by, counted by a cheap plastic clock on the wall which I refused to look at. It wouldn't move if I looked at it. That was just how the clocks seemed to work at school. If you did some work and looked at it, you had a chance of getting lucky and seeing that half an hour had passed. But if you just kept looking, it'd decide to pretend to be a snail. Clocks were weird like that.

"Alright, five minutes of lunch left! Let's get this room back to how it was when we came in—I'm looking at you three, don't just disappear!"

The three Year 7s protested a little but still dragged the furniture back to its proper positions. I stood as my chair was eyed up for moving by one of them, barely grabbing my bag from under it before it was snatched away. They could be strangely enthusiastic about anything. Mrs Linn probably helped—if she tried, she could make exams fun.

But summer still loomed over me like the darkest cloud I'd ever seen, ready to burst into a downpour of dirty, grey rain at any moment. I couldn't do anything. Nova's phone was away, firmly tucked into a blazer pocket. Everyone was gravitating towards the door, waiting for Mrs Linn to say the room was fine and they—we—could leave. This was my only outlet (which I never used), my only safe space (which I was too scared to participate in) and the only place where I ever felt like I could be myself.

It was crumbling away before my eyes, but I could do nothing to stop it.

Giving up, I trudged towards the door, waiting to leave with everyone else. No one noticed me. No one looked up as I approached. Just like a ghost, I drifted through the group without a word. Sometimes, it was almost like people looked through me.

I might've been acting a little melodramatic, but I truly felt miserable.

"Ay, Charlie," shocked to the core, I spun around to see Nova peering down at me, brushing a floppy fringe out of their face, "did I get your Insta? Or do I already follow you?"

"I-um-it's-" words became mush in my mouth, sticking to my tongue.

"I am following you! Never mind, never mind, I'll add you now—sorry about that, God, can't believe I forgot. See you next year!"

Sweeping past me, they left through the door which Mrs Linn was holding open, disappearing before I could form a proper sentence. I gulped down a lump which had made its home in my throat. Almost numb with a mix of surprise and nervousness, I wandered out into the corridor and tried to remember what my next lesson was.

∞

Getting a buzzing notification for 'Gay Group 2: The Online One' was the best feeling in the world, even if it did happen half-way through a surprise maths quiz. Can't have everything, I guess.

Advice

35% of LGBT students have an LGBT group at their school. (Stonewall, 2017)

LGBT+ groups or clubs can be a lifesaver at high school and college. They can connect you with new friends who understand who you are and how you identify and give you tips on how to live as a young LGBT+ person in a world which is not always great at accepting us. Like any group, they're also fun and a nice place to relax. Getting away from the stress of ordinary life for even half an hour can really help you out on tough days.

But, as with everything, they're not always perfect. In some schools and colleges, they may not even exist. You might not be aware of them, or you might be targeted for going to them. There are plenty of risks which come with identifying yourself with an LGBT+ group and I'm not going to sugar-coat that. If your school or college has a private, secure LGBT+ group for you, then that's great—I attend such a group myself (in an obviously private location). But I've also gone to a group which was completely out-in-the-open and treated like any other club. Both choices have pros and cons, but the bottom line is to listen to yourself and your gut. You don't have to go to an LGBT+ group just because your school decided to open one; it's entirely your call to make.

The benefits of making LGBT+ friends are pretty unique, though, so, if you don't have an LGBT+

group at school, what can you do? There's a couple of answers. You could make an unofficial group yourself if you're up for the responsibility, either in-person or online. You could reach out to your school or college and ask them to consider creating one. Or you could find an online community of LGBT+ people to join. Obviously, you have to be careful whenever you're online, but if you take the proper precautions (no personal or identifying details, no agreements to meet with strangers, no bank details given out, etc.) it can be a supportive experience.

Resources

Websites

https://www.consortium.lgbt/member-directory - a website full of LGBT+ groups in the UK.
https://www.trevorspace.org - an online community for LGBT+ youth.

Will You Go--

Content Warnings

Homophobic Language
Homophobic Bullying

Holly, she/her

I have a crush on Beth.

I know, terrible way to start a story, right? But it's true. That beautiful girl, sitting across from me in the stuffy old school library, is everything. We spend breaks and lunch together, every day, and we walk home with our hands so close to each other that I have to bite my tongue not to reach out and hold hers. Crazy, right?

This lunchtime is going to be different. I can feel it. Sure, Miss Instant-Noodle-Hair (not her real name, but Miss Ashton sounds boring in comparison) is looming over us, wandering around the reception desk like a mother duck looking for her little lost ducklings, but that's fine. Some loud Year 9s are trying to play cards in the corner, the stakes seeming to be chocolate-based, but that's fine. Even the Year 7s screaming at jump scares from whatever game they're playing on the library computers doesn't bother me.

Not today. Today is different.

Today I'm going to ask Beth out.

"You can't tell me I'm wrong!" Madison's surprisingly loud declaration brings me out of my thoughts and brings Miss Instant-Noodle-Hair a little closer. Her eyes seem to watch everyone at once. "There's literally no evidence against my theory!"

"There's also none *for* your theory," Beth, a brunette goddess in a tacky, mustard-yellow uniform which even she can't pull off (it's impossible—plenty of people have tried to make it look fashionable, to no avail), shakes her head and smiles.

That smile... it would light up the room, but the strip electric lights glaring down at us already do that.

"Exactly! Wait—"

All three of us laugh, Miss Instant-Noodle-Hair moving on to tell off the Year 9s. For some reason, she seems more concerned with their noise than their obvious gambling, but that's high school for you.

Anyway, there's a small problem with my crush on Beth. Well, I say 'small', but it's actually been clawing into my back like a mountain-sized monster, or the fear of homework deadlines and exams, for weeks. It's not that we're already close friends, or that we're young and I'm worried about the prospect of having a proper relationship for the first time. No, it's worse than all of that.

Beth's a girl; she's a wonderful, stunning, intelligent, confident girl.

But so am I.

Not the whole 'stunning' and 'confident' bit, but the 'girl' part is very important. I... well, I guess I'm a lesbian, or definitely some sort of girl-loving person. I haven't got it all figured out yet.

But Beth? It's a mystery.

Trust me, I've tried to work it out. Mentioning pride events just segues us into conversations about the musicians who perform at them. Gay celebrities? Somehow, we end up moving onto the TV shows and movies they've been in. I tried bringing up a book with a gay couple in it, only to be lectured on the writing style and plot elements, or something like that.

I tried to listen. I always do when she starts talking about things she loves. Seeing her face light up with enthusiasm is amazing.

"I'm just saying, we both have two eyes, mouths—" Madison starts again, only to be shot down immediately.

"Have you ever seen a human with gills?" Trying to talk seriously for a moment, Beth holds her hand over her mouth, hiding the smile which I unabashedly adore.

"That's beside the point."

"That's the entire point!"

For some reason, in the laughter break which follows Beth's exasperated words, I feel fate and destiny take me by the hand. *This is it*, they whisper, *this is it. It's your moment.* I don't have to ask what the moment is for. It's been on my mind all lunchtime —all day—all week. All month.

"Hey, Beth, will you go—"

Before the last of my adrenaline-fuelled words can pass through my lips, I'm interrupted. Rudely.

"Lesbos," he passes in a moment, a blur of a black non-school-uniform-compliant rain jacket and a curly hair cut.

A long, long minute passes between us. A minute which drives us closer to our next lessons. A minute which I could've spent asking Beth out. A minute which some random guy decided to ruin for no reason.

Great.

Fate and destiny are no longer my best friends. Not that they really were, I guess, but now they're definitely not.

"We're not even lesbians," Madison sighs, dropping her head on the table between us—the thud alerts Miss Instant-Noodle-Hair, but one of the Year 9s wins a round of cards and his celebrations draw her away, "why are people so stupid?"

"He thinks he's funny, doesn't matter to him if we're gay or not," shaking her head, Beth pats Madison's dark, springy hair softly before looking to me, "you alright, Holly?"

"Fine," my reply spits its way through gritted teeth.

That was my moment. My intertwining of destiny and fate. My decision to risk our friendship for love. It was all mine, but he had to steal it for a quick joke.

If he thinks three girls hanging out together is some sort of code for identifying as lesbian, he must be horrified by the canteen.

But I can't dwell on it. Before Beth can figure out that something is wrong, I force a smile and prompt Madison back into the fish-human-debate, despite not really listening to it before. Something about humans evolving from fish—that's about as scientific as our friend group gets, I'm afraid.

Soon enough, there's a messy diagram of a fish-human-hybrid which would probably make our biology teacher faint on the table, wriggly lines scribbled on notebook paper with a chewed biro.

Doing my best to look like I'm studying the recent addition to Madison's 'theory', my mind travels back to that interrupted question. 'Will you go —'... Well, I guess it ended there. Is it some sort of sign from fate and destiny? Have they changed their minds? Or is it some sort of test, to see if I really want to ask Beth out?

Do I really want to ask Beth out?

We're steaming through Year 11 (far too fast for my liking), getting close to GCSEs and picking colleges. We might get split up. None of us have really thought about it too much. But I have thought about her, for months now. It barely feels like months. Every day blurs into one long daydream of her soft face, the round cheeks and the eyelashes she delicately paints with mascara every morning. Tests and homework fade into the background. TV shows and movies pale in comparison.

I don't want to ask her out. I *need* to.

"In conclusion, I'm right and everyone else in the world is wrong!" Looking proud of herself, Madison waves the scrappy bit of paper in my face, waking me up once more. I really need to start paying attention to reality. It would make sense to, considering that I have to live in it. "Right, Holly?"

"I mean, if 'everyone else in the world is wrong', then me saying you're right makes you wrong," confusing even myself with that sentence, I smile triumphantly, nonetheless. Madison stares at me, cogs turning in her head.

"I think she's got you beat," Beth says, my cheeks heating up before I can flop a sleeve in front of them, "and—oh, great. Guess who's here."

Considering her tone, I really don't need to. I don't even look. He won't say it again. He's not stupid—well, he might be, but hopefully he's not that stupid. Fate taps me on the shoulder, but I know the games that supernatural forces play. Destiny tries to whisper in my ear. Ignoring them, I cast my eyes down to the sad creature on Madison's paper, a rigid, drawn-on grin failing to improve the overall impression of pitifulness.

"He's got friends," Madison murmurs, making me roll my eyes. Of course he does. My day just can't get any worse, can it?

Will you go out with me? Fate and destiny are having a laugh. All of a sudden, my head is full of whirling words. I can't escape. It almost feels like some sort of tug of war, with one person wanting me to ask and another yanking the opportunity away. They give me the words and take away the chance to use them.

Will you go out with me? It lingers on the tip of my tongue, threatening to fall off at any moment and sneak into Beth's ear. My insides are being torn apart.

Ask, don't ask. Wait, don't wait. Leave it, do it now.

Whoever decided that today would be the day I'd get royally messed with by the entire universe is going to feel my wrath—as soon as I get away from this table, this lunchtime and this stupid guy who thinks he's a comedian.

With an entourage, of course, because one of him just wasn't enough.

"You're all dirty lesbos, you," this time, his stupid comment is followed by stupid tittering from his stupid friends, who I really hate right now. Fate and destiny can take a back seat; I have stupid Year-whatever-they-ares to deal with.

This, of course, is a terrible idea, but I started this story terribly so I might as well follow through.

"WILL YOU GO OUT WITH ME?"

Not my greatest moment. With just a quick overview, we can see exactly where I went wrong a few seconds ago. See, leaping up in the middle of the library and screaming is a great way to attract the attention of Miss Instant-Noodle-Hair, who is now storming over with a face of pure thunder.

Screaming that particular question at a curly-haired boy who just called you and all your friends 'dirty lesbos' is a wonderful way to get a lot of confused looks from him and his cronies pretty quickly, before the disgusted expressions and 'ew's set in. You know what's the worst of all, though?

When the girl you actually wanted to ask out has just been deafened by you and is now sitting in stunned silence.

Yeah, it's funny how a load of terrible things

happen in high school. Just ask Madison. She's always the first to bring up the time I got stuck in a toilet cubicle, finally getting rescued by a PE teacher and a senior member of staff, but not after I inadvertently filled the toilets to bursting with a curious crowd. I've got a few about her, though, and Beth too. It's all equal.

At least none of us set the fire alarm off in the pouring rain—that honour (and the undying hatred of absolutely everyone in this school) goes to Will from Year 8.

I'm sure everything will be forgotten by the time we're adults, with jobs and families and whatever else adults have. Well, maybe not Will, but everything else is almost one hundred percent forgettable.

This, though? I'm not really sure.

With Miss Instant-Noodle-Hair closing in, I jump up and kick my chair away for good measure. Not-at-all-good-tip, if you decide to suddenly become rebellious and angry, go all out! Never follow that rule. Ever. It's also called digging a hole for yourself, and it's not generally looked upon as wise.

But I grab my shovel and push everyone out of the way and run outside to dig my hole anyway because I've spent fifteen years on this earth and none of them taught me how to deal with whatever just happened calmly and logically.

No, my brain just went 'let's go', so we went.

Cold air and common sense hit me in the face

in the corridor. Regret comes, in waves of 'what have you just done' and 'that was so cool' and 'you just ruined your entire life' and 'let's do it again'. They're some pretty choppy waves.

Kids walk past, not even pretending they're not staring. I don't really blame them. My cheeks feel hotter than that tray in cooking class which I forgot in the oven for an hour (another funny story Madison loves to tell). There might be tears in my eyes, but they're not falling down my cheeks. Instead, they're being a nuisance and clouding my vision. Everything is against me today, it seems.

My ears don't even pick up on the library door opening and closing, quietly. Carefully. I don't hear the gentle footsteps on the corridor. I don't notice the girl I call a goddess padding up to my side, eyes large and kind and full of some sort of wonder.

I figure it out when I turn around and nearly have a heart attack at the sight of her.

"Tryna kill me, sneaking up on me like that?" Mock-angry, I wave a hand around, pretending to have more energy than I really do. That altercation took everything out of me. She only smiles.

"You can't fool me with that delicate act, not after that," she gestures towards the library with her head, prompting another gushing of blood into my cheeks, "but I'm glad you can still joke around after that rejection."

"I wasn't trying to ask him out," I groan, my head hitting the wall behind me, "I don't even know his name."

"You know my name."

Is that... is that...

Is it happening?

Fate nods. Destiny smirks. This was their plan all along.

Stupid plan. What's wrong with a simple, non-embarrassing love story?

"Beth—Beth," throat dry and palms clammy, I try to get those crucial words out, "will you go—" no interruption, not this time, just vague crowds of kids drifting past and the x-ray glare of Miss Instant-Noodle-Hair, but she has no power here, "will you go out with me?"

A smile. A soft hand, interlocking fingers with mine. A nod.

My goddess has taken me to heaven.

Advice

45% of lesbian, gay, bisexual and trans students are bullied for being LGBT at school. (Stonewall, 2017)

Unfortunately, bullying is a common problem for many people in high school, especially if you're spotted being 'different' for whatever reason. That reason may be being LGBT+, since high school kids aren't always nice and accepting of other identities. But when you're being bullied, what can you do? It can sometimes feel like you're all alone, even if you've got friends around you, so the first step is to take a deep breath and reach out to the people you care about and who care about you. Their support might give you the confidence to go through the next, more tricky steps.

If it's happening in school or college, go to a teacher or staff member that you trust. It could be your form tutor, a subject teacher or even a head of year. Their job is not only to educate you but also to keep you happy and safe. It might feel terrifying to actually go up to them and ask for help, but it's one of your best options. Parents or guardians and other trusted adults like youth workers are also good people to reach out to and have open conversations with about what's been going on.

But bullying doesn't always happen within school hours. In this case, assess your situation and respond accordingly. Are you in immediate danger? Call the police's emergency line. Has an incident (such as being called slurs) happened but you're safe now? Call the police's non-emergency line. Your school may still be able to help if the bully[ies] also attend it but contacting the police to make sure that things don't escalate may be needed. Bullying is never your fault; don't feel like a burden if you reach out for help, because you deserve to feel happy and safe.

Resources

Websites

https://www.letsendhatecrime.com - (Greater Manchester) if bullying escalates to hate crime, you can report it here (and also learn what exactly a hate crime is).
https://www.stophateuk.org/report-lgb-and-t-hate-crime/ - report LGBTQI+ hate crime and hate incidents.
https://www.kooth.com - a supportive online community with live chat well-being services.
https://www.childline.org.uk/ - Childline website.

Hotlines

999 - police emergency line.
101 - police non-emergency line.
0800 1111 – Childline hotline.

Smoke Rings & Pride Flags

*Smoke Rings & Pride Flags first appeared in
Potted Purple Mag*

Content Warnings

Tobacco Use
Underage Tobacco Use
Electronic Cigarette Use
Underage Electronic Cigarette Use
Peer Pressure
Mention Of Cancer
Unsupportive Family

Jason, he/him

"Right, it's chill-out time—if you're going outside, please be respectful of the general public and the building."

As a struggle over who got to connect to the speaker began, I moved my chair back and stood up hesitantly. Outside seemed like a good idea. The meeting-room, although large enough, got really hot with thirty or so people sitting around talking about plans for the local pride event and other campaigns they were starting. I'd listened until darkness cloaked the outside world. There were blinds over the windows (for our safety, it was stressed) but little slithers of the street managed to get through them.

Streetlights blinked on. Cars growled past with their headlights on full blast. Loud, drunken conversations fought through the closed windows and assaulted our group.

Our group. Could I even say that yet? This was my first session, after all. I'd been promised a safe space to make friends and get involved with local projects, and it had been provided for me tonight. But there I was, getting up and sidling out of the roasting room without a second glance at the youth workers in their rainbow lanyards and the kids fighting over the music.

I left before I could hear who won.

A small crowd of blurry faces, too new to be recognisable yet, rushed out as if they never wanted to be there in the first place. I knew better, though.

The one with the blue hair had debated another person on school policies, and leather jacket guy was full of ideas for the pride float. At the time, they had loved being there, and being a part of it all.

But as soon as 'chill-out' time was announced, their chairs were thrown back, bags grabbed, and doors wrenched open. All of them filed into the corridor with the locked door (locked on one side but not the other), which had a little red button for releasing people into the reception area. They took turns jabbing the button and yelling at each other to open the door until there was only one person left.

It took me a while to realise he was looking straight at me since my eyes had been busy exploring the boring tiled floor.

"Are you coming out, or staying here?" A simple question. His voice was a little rough, but not unkind. Sort of down-to-earth, if that made sense. It was the sort of voice you trusted with your life, but not your chocolate. "Jason, right? New?"

"Y-yeah, that's, that's me," realising, with a little mix of horror and embarrassment, that I couldn't remember his name from the introductions, I was stuck hoping he wouldn't notice without being able to do anything about it, "I'm gonna—well, I was gonna go out, I guess—"

"Great. Press the button."

Cutting me off, he started striding towards the door. Still stumbling over useless words, I looked towards the red button. A little bit of plastic had never looked so intimidating. It was only the fact that I'd never pressed it before which made it intimidating, of course, but it still seemed to threaten me, sat there on the wall. No, it was smug. *You won't press me. You can't.*

"Press the button," he repeated, a little more firmly this time, so I pressed it.

With a grunt, he flung open the heavy-looking door and walked straight through it, leaving me to wonder if he'd just abandon me. That thought lasted for about half a second. The door never swung shut, since he was holding it open, like some sort of polite gentleman. He certainly didn't look the part, but I wasn't about to complain.

"Thanks, uh," still not sure of what my tongue was trying to do, I hurried forwards, almost scared he'd shut the door in my face. He didn't, of course, because people are rarely as bad as you think they'll be. Most have some sort of sense of decency. Especially if they hold a door open for you.

"My name's Leo. You weren't listening through intros—try not to make a habit of it," he let the door go, putting a hand on my shoulder and leading me towards the revolving doors which were between us and 'outside'.

'Outside' was a crowd of teenagers, some sitting, some standing and some running about like little kids, with smoke puffing out of them like they were a gathering of steam trains. It was straight out of a warning poster from school, 'don't ruin your life with these losers', or something a little more subtle than that. A lump formed in my throat.

But we kept moving, Leo's supportive hand still on my shoulder. It fell away as we waited for the revolving door to let out a dad and his two tiny children, one of them coughing hysterically. From the way he was telling the kid off, I reckoned it was just an act, but I couldn't blame them. There was practically a smokescreen outside.

It was only when we passed through the door and stepped out into the night that Leo's hand returned, and I realised I kind of liked the warmth of his touch on my shoulder. Not in a romantic way, or a crush way, but just an 'I've got you, follow me' way, if that made sense. It was nice. After a day of following around 'friends' who didn't really talk to me and a silent car ride with my disapproving parents, it was a breath of fresh air.

Unfortunately, that was only a metaphor. The actual air outside was fruit and tobacco flavoured. Oh—and bubblegum. Wonderful.

It wasn't that I had anything against smokers (or vapers, for that matter). It just didn't appeal to me. Getting force-fed second-hand candy-clouds also didn't appeal to me, but I don't think asking them to 'keep the smoke down' would've done anything. My tongue would probably mess up the words anyway.

The building had a little paved section between it and the next big brick block—it was a library if I remembered correctly, but the shutters were down and I didn't have a chance to get a proper look at the name printed above them.

Benches were placed directly down the middle, with ash-covered bins by every single one. A streetlight flickered in the centre of everything.

Despite having all of this room, the teenage crowd chose to huddle against the glass wall of the building, seeming to irritate a few receptionists within it. For some reason, I didn't think this was what the youth worker had in mind when he said to 'be respectful' of the surroundings.

"Oi, Leo! You adopted the new kid or something?"

Leo paused to turn and face the fiercely smoking crowd, an easy smile on his face. I was less calm. My heart decided to try and go for a record of beats per minute, and my ribs decided to make every single pulse echo around my entire body. My body seemed to sink into itself, air freezing in my lungs and holding me in some sort of stasis.

"Get him over here, we'll take care of him!"

"You'll shove a cig down his throat, you idiot. Acting like I haven't watched you corrupt every one of these," Leo waved generally at the crowd, who laughed or yelled obscenities back, "nah. I'll keep his lungs clean."

"Mr Stingy over here'll never let you have a smoke," the speaker was coming closer—it was the blue-haired person—grinning and pulling out a vomit-coloured, rectangular box, "but I will, lad. Come hang with us."

A single orange-and-white cigarette was pulled from the box. It dangled between Blue-hair's long fingers. Brief temptation flitted through my mind.

I could... but why would I? I didn't really want to take it. Disease and another reason for my parents to hate me didn't sound like the best idea.

But another terrifying thought lingered in my head—how exactly did I refuse him when my tongue refused to work?

"Give me that," Leo rolled his eyes and grabbed the cigarette, taking me by the shoulder again and moving me away from the now-protesting Blue-hair, "what? You were gonna give it away anyway!"

"Not to you!"

The crowd erupted into a wave of laughter, but I didn't look back at them. I couldn't. My head was fixed in one position: forwards. I'd get used to them eventually, I was sure, but right then they were all as scary as monsters under the bed used to be. Or still were, on some nights, but that was a secret.

Leo led me towards one of the benches, sitting us down on the cold metal without a word. There was still a smile on his face as he shook his head and passed the cigarette between his hands. I stayed quiet, not knowing what to say. The crowd were making enough noise for the entire town, so I suppose I didn't really need to say anything at all.

"Jason," he began, reaching into his pocket but looking me in the eyes, "promise me," a neon orange lighter appeared in his hand, staying still in the air for a moment, "that you'll never smoke."

"Are you... are you joking?" I asked cautiously, as he proceeded to put the orange end of the cigarette between his lips and begin clicking the lighter. It didn't seem to be working very well, but a little flame appeared a few seconds later, licking the white paper and turning it black. He breathed in heavily, turned his head and blew the white-grey smoke away. "You're smoking."

"And it's bad for you, so you shouldn't do it," he returned, shrugging, the smile gone from his face, "don't listen to Kai. He's an idiot. An idiot who's gonna get lung cancer one day and wish he gave all his cigs away."

"Are they all idiots?" I don't really know why that question left my throat, but it did. It made him laugh. The laugh turned into a cough after a mistimed drag from the cigarette, so I patted his back gently, likely having no impact. The coughing stopped, but he kept smiling.

"Yup, and you're an idiot for coming here. For coming outside, anyway," when he noticed I wasn't laughing with him, he shook his head and patted my shoulder, "that was a joke, Jase—can I call you that? Rolls off the tongue nicer than Jason, doesn't it?"

"I—if you want to, I guess," I nodded, not really minding what he called me as long as it wasn't some sort of insult.

Even though he just invented a nickname for me, he didn't speak for a little while after that. My eyes wandered over to the boisterous crowd, who had started clapping as one of them ran around with a pride flag draped over their back like a cape. It was the non-binary flag, if I wasn't mistaken (which I might've been).

My own identity wasn't new to me but knowing the name for it and simply the fact that the rest of the community existed was a bit of a surprise a couple of years ago. I blamed a sheltered upbringing and religious schools which didn't want to utter the word 'gay' in case all their students suddenly 'caught the gay', or something ridiculous like that.

None of this is real, Jason, you've got to remember that. It'll all be over in a few months, so stop messing around.

Where did that come from? Startled, I looked around, almost expecting my mum's tired, disappointed face to appear out of nowhere. Instead, a chilling wind decided to invade my hoodie, forcing goosebumps to pop up all over my arms. I could feel every single one. Being inside that warm meeting room didn't seem so bad anymore.

I'm not talking about this now. Don't bring it up again.

She'd said that a million times, but it never stopped her talking about it. Dad didn't talk about it, but he never really talked about anything. For years, I'd tried to get him into all sorts of conversations, even venturing into the few interests of his that I knew (various sports, the outrageous fact that prices sometimes went up at his favourite supermarket and half marathons) but he never really responded.

Sometimes, he spoke to my friends more than me, but that might've just been him being polite.

I hadn't gotten the chance to test that out recently, since all my friends seemed to suddenly take after him and lose all their interest in me. It was awful when I thought about it, but it happened so gradually that I barely realised at the time. One day, people stopped laughing at my jokes. By the next week, they didn't look at me if I talked. Another week and I was being talked over.

Quickly, I learned to keep quiet and just follow them around.

"So, what are you here for?" Incredibly grateful for Leo's question, I leapt out of my depressing thoughts and rushed to find an answer for him.

"I'm bisexual!" For a few seconds, I didn't understand why he was laughing. I didn't really mind —his laughter was nice to listen to, just like his voice but with an added helping of joy. Then, it hit me.

"Thanks for telling me, but I sort of meant 'I'm here to make friends' or 'I'm here to change the world'," he used air quotes for each little reason, "like, I'm here because a youth worker dragged me here. 'Beneficial for my mental health', or something like that. So, wanna try that again?"

"I—uh, they came into school. Shirley and Mike," he nodded, so I kept going, "and, at the end of the assembly, I sort of went and asked if I could join. I think—I think I just wanted to make friends."

"Support system," he said knowingly, taking

another drag from the half-gone cigarette, "that makes sense. You automatically have something in common with everyone here. Even those lot," he pointed his cigarette at the crowd, who had started arguing over who got to wear the pride flag, "if you can believe it. Yeah, that's fair enough. You'll fit in just fine, give it a couple weeks."

"Did you..." not really knowing how to phrase the question, I thought for a few seconds, giving Leo the chance to take a long, long drag on his cigarette, before puffing out something which looked sort of like a deformed ring, "did you feel scared, or sort of alone, when you first came here?"

"I mean, I was here when it all started, so everyone was a bit new and nervous," his eyes became a little distant, maybe looking into memories from long ago, "it's probably worse for you, joining when everyone already knows each other. It's the difference between going from primary to high school and going to a new school in the middle of the year, you know?"

"That makes sense," I leaned back onto the bench a little, regretting it as the cold metal sent a chill through my back. Leo glanced over.

"Bring a coat next week," he advised me, the knowledgeable tone back in his voice.

Casually, he draped his arm around me.

Blinking a little, I wondered what to do for a second. It only took that second for my nervousness to be shouted over by a need for warmth. Leaning my head onto his chest, I fell into a warm embrace which smelled like cigarettes and the boys' changing rooms at school: cheap deodorant. Somewhat reassuringly, there was nothing 'else' about the interaction—no roaming hands, no close face, no whispered words. Just a hug. A sideways hug, but a hug nonetheless.

I hadn't been hugged in years.

He continued to finish his cigarette, sometimes remarking that 'so-and-so' was underage and shouldn't have been smoking at all (there were quite a few 'so-and-so's) and that 'they' used to be in a relationship but had a messy breakup, or that Shirley always made jokes about Mike's weird ties, especially at Christmas and Halloween. Any holiday, he said, or any day of the week when Mike decided pink and green polka dots were in fashion.

"Do me a favour," putting the end of his cigarette out in the bin's ashtray, he looked down at me with a serious expression, "and never, ever listen to Kai. Well, you can listen to him, 'cause he can be funny sometimes, but never take him seriously. He's a good comedian and a bad influence."

"Why'd he call you 'Mr Stingy'?" Instead of actually replying to the question, I decided to ask something which had been on my mind ever since my encounter with Kai.

"I never give him cigs. Or anyone else." Leo shrugged.

"Because you don't want them to smoke?"

"Nah. I just can't afford it. Smoking's an expensive habit, y'know."

For the first time that day, I genuinely laughed. Leo started too, his chest shaking with every chuckle, and I was filled with the wonderful feeling of friendship. Sure, I'd only known him for half an hour at most, but he'd decided to make my first day at that group better. He'd made me feel welcome, something which even the youth workers and their friendly smiles couldn't manage.

Pulling his phone out of his pocket with his free hand, he near-blinded me with the white electric glare of his home screen. A band I didn't know flipped me off from behind the time: 19:56. Almost time for everything to end; almost time for that awkward car ride home.

I knew the only reason my parents allowed me to go to the group was because of Shirley's home-visit, required for every new member of the group, which had been a lot of persuading and highlighting the 'benefits', without directly calling them out for anything. Being a youth worker seemed to take a lot of skill.

But even Shirley couldn't stop their disapproving looks and critical silence.

"Remember a coat next week," Leo told me, a gentle smile on his face, "and stay as far away from Kai as you can. Got it?"

"Yeah," chewing my lip, I considered asking him something which had bubbled to the surface of my mind, his friendly expression inviting me to say the words: "do you, uh—can I sit next to you? Next week?" Picking a seat had been one of the most nerve-wracking experiences of my life, sending adrenaline pumping around my body as I desperately searched for Shirley. Luckily, the seat next to her was available, but I didn't really want to repeat the process next week.

"Sure, Jase. Just find me in reception, I'm always here early."

"Thanks," my words were covered in relief, a real smile curving up my lips.

Maybe everything else in my week would be rubbish, but at least I could look forward to this.

Advice

People who identify as gay or lesbian are approximately 1.4 times more likely to smoke than people who identify as straight. (ONS, 2018)

Smoking is not smart. It's not cool, or funny, or edgy, or whatever else. It's putting poison in your lungs and you'll regret it later in life. But that doesn't erase the fact that young people *do* smoke and that LGBT+ people seem to be slightly more likely to smoke. So, if you find yourself in a situation where all your friends are smoking and you don't know if you should join them, what should you do?

First of all, if there's any doubt in your mind about smoking—if you're worried about your health, your parents or even the smell—that's a sign that you shouldn't be doing it. If anything, it'll just make you worry about the consequences, which definitely isn't fun. But it can be tough to turn down your friends. Remember, though, if your friends think less of you for not smoking then they're not great friends. You can always find different people to hang out with, or spend your time doing different hobbies and activities instead of mindlessly sitting in a park/forest/outside the school gates (some likely 'youth smoking areas').

Still, you might've already started smoking. Is it too late? Nope. Quitting at any time is better than continuing, especially when you're younger. You can get advice online or speak to a school nurse if you're struggling with quitting—don't feel bad if you are, because it is a difficult thing to do. Try and make new, non-smoking friends or talk more to your old, non-smoking friends. Above all, just don't smoke. It's not worth it.

Resources

Websites

https://www.nhs.uk/live-well/quit-smoking/nhs-stop-smoking-services-help-you-quit/ - NHS help to stop smoking.
https://www.nhs.uk/live-well/quit-smoking/quitting-smoking-under-18s-guide/ - NHS youth help to stop smoking.
https://www.blf.org.uk/take-action/campaign-with-us/stoptober - Stoptober (stop smoking for October) information.

Hotlines

0300 123 1044 – England, Smokefree National Helpline, Free.
0800 84 84 84 – Scotland, Smokeline, Free.
0800 085 2219 – Wales, Help Me Quit, Free.
https://www.stopsmokingni.info/ways-quit/local-help-and-support - Northern Ireland, Stop Smoking, Hotlines by Address, Free.

It Itches In The Dark

Content Warnings

Horror Imagery
Chest-Related Gender Dysphoria
Self-Harm Intrusive Thoughts
Mention Of Gender Clinic Waiting Lists
Mention Of Mental Health Services (Therapy)

IT ITCHES IN THE DARK

Cyrus, he/him

12 AM. The alarm clock leers at me in glaring red. Harsh, rigid numbers look down at me without any pity. *You want to sleep?* They ask. *You're tired? Too bad.* They don't care about my 9 AM college classes or the homework I need to do at some point before tomorrow. Tomorrow, or today?

I hate being up this late. It's too confusing.

Darkness hangs over everything in my tiny box room, the shadows haunting every nook and cranny. Monsters, I used to call them, when I was small and... well, when I was small and different. That thought brings everything full circle.

There are ants underneath my skin, gnawing at my chest. The chest covered in two lumps which I don't want or need.

Get rid of them. Some voice inside me thinks it's being original, as if I haven't had this itch for years. It takes every bit of willpower inside me to keep my fingernails secure in two balled fists. They want nothing more than to be let loose on that saggy flesh. They want to cut. Tear. Scratch.

These things don't belong on me. They're not mine. I don't know where they came from. Puberty hit and dysphoria decided to follow it, barely giving me a chance to keep up. One minute I started bleeding every month, the next I had breasts. Boys don't bleed every month. Boys don't have breasts.

Well, I guess they do. I do, at least.

Closing my eyes, I breathe in deeply.

My name is Cyrus. My name is Cyrus. My name is Cyrus.

It's a chant my therapist taught me, the only useful thing she's ever done. The name kicks whatever part of me is sad about having female features and reminds me that I'm a boy on the inside. Not really the inside, I guess, but the inside-inside. The place that counts.

My next step is a tip from the internet, which has been a blessing compared to Jill. Jill sits on a comfy chair and scribbles down notes in her terrible handwriting, nodding and humming and 'oh that's so sad'-ing for an hour every month. The internet, on the other hand, has memes. Oh, and tips for dealing with gender dysphoria, but mainly memes.

Relaxing one fist into an open palm, I bring it up to just between my collarbones. Then, down. The fingers drift, exploring the flat space between the two bags of fat I hate. As long as the hand doesn't go left or right, I can almost kid myself into thinking that the waiting list for top surgery has suddenly disappeared and I've already been under the knife. Or scalpel. I don't really understand that phrase.

The peace doesn't last. I have to clench the fist again to stop my fingernails getting anywhere near my breasts. Down it goes, until both my hands are firmly at my sides and I'm staring up at a ceiling which may or may not be covered in childhood shadow monsters. It isn't, I don't think, but you never know.

Dysphoria feels like a monster inside of my

chest, scratching to get out. Or is that my 'boy-self', if there is such a thing? Thinking about an actual person being trapped inside of my actual body is a bit frightening. I can see it now, in some sort of horror TV show. It'll escape through the mouth, but not before it reaches out of those jaws with long, spider-like hands, the fingers twisting and scratching. Ugh. I need to sleep before I turn into that monster.

Or am I already the monster? I've forgotten already.

12.04 AM. I can't believe it's only been four minutes. I'm not complaining—realising that five hours have slipped through your fingers after bingeing a good TV show is terrifying. But still, only four minutes?

Wait, never mind.

12.05 AM.

It's been five minutes. I'm not going back to sleep any time soon, but I also can't stand just lying here and doing nothing. The suffocating darkness really isn't helping either. I could bother someone and text them, or call them, but everyone should be asleep, considering everyone has college tomorrow. *I* also have college tomorrow.

But there's no point in waking them up too.

Rolling out of bed, I end up in a tangled heap of arms, legs and duvet on the thankfully-carpeted floor. Cheap carpet, but it's better than nothing.

I yawn. I kick away the duvet. I roll around a bit more, just for good measure, then get up and feel dizzy for no reason. Except maybe the rolling around, but I'm too tired to make rational connections between events that just happened. No, I've got a new purpose in life.

~~Go to sleep.~~

Go to the bathroom.

It's not a grand purpose, but it'll do. The door handle is cold on my fingers, but I'm past caring. My door opens with a whine, begging for some grease or oil or whatever you put on noisy hinges. It'll have to wait. A dark corridor is greeting me, pulling me into a cold draft and reminding me that I'm completely naked.

I hope Mum doesn't suddenly wake up and need to visit the toilet.

Reaching out with one hand, I find the wall and use it to guide my tired eyes towards the bathroom. I firmly believe that I'm completely useless after 9 PM. I turn into some sort of zombie, falling into everything with water leaking out of my eyes for absolutely no reason. Wires become traps. Pets become enemies. Parents become NPCs I can't be bothered talking to.

It's fine. Mum and Laura know I love them—I say it enough before 9 PM to make up for my midnight brain-death.

Attempting not to create any loud noises, I make my way into the dark bathroom. It's almost as big as my room, which is probably pretty good for the bathroom but not great for me. *Close the door, find the lights.* Lights on. I'm blinded for a few seconds.

A few seconds turn into a minute. Yeah, I'm really bad at functioning after-dark. Really, really bad. Eventually, some sort of reflection starts staring at me, and it takes me half a minute to figure out that it's me. Once I figure it out, I frown. It's not me.

I don't mean that it's some sort of ghostly figure from a horror movie in the mirror, just that my physical appearance drastically mismatches with how I 'see' myself. There's a stronger jawline in my head, broader shoulders and a prominent Adam's apple. Stubble. An average-sized penis.

A flat chest.

Instead of all that, I get... this. Feminine. A stomach that sticks out a bit. Two fatty bits of rubbish where a flat chest should be. A remarkable absence of any male genitalia. Noodle arms and barely existent shoulders. Purple bags under eyes with long eyelashes and a small nose. I don't know why I'm bothered about the nose—I don't think I am, to be honest. Everything just muddles together and slaps my brain with word mush.

Bad. Bad body. Body not male. Get rid. Scratch. Scratch it now. Do it. Why did you have to be born this way?

Sure, I can get rid of it all. I can change it. After years and years of waiting lists and referrals and who-knows-what-else—bureaucratic nonsense which means I haven't even got hormones yet because I was referred too late for the children's gender service but too early for the adult one.

Years. It makes my eyes water when I think about it for too long. I've been screaming for help, but everyone just shoves you away and makes you someone else's problem.

How many more times do I have to say 'I'm a boy' for someone to actually do something?

This is where staying up late gets me. Stood in a bathroom, freezing and crying silently. They're the weird tears, the ones that run down your face and make your eyes look ugly, even though the tears themselves look quite neat and orderly. They taste salty. Then they mix with nose-mucus and taste like snot.

Itch. Itch. Itch. I've never wanted to do anything more than I want to itch right now. I know I can't. It'll just make the skin an angry red colour and leave my fingernails with disgusting little bits of skin stuck in them. It won't solve anything. I physically won't be able to bring myself to scratch my breasts off—even the idea sounds ridiculous.

But it doesn't stop the itching. It doesn't stop the ants racing around beneath the lumps I detest. Nothing can stop it. Nothing *I* can do, anyway. I can hide them under blankets and a binder and baggy t-shirts and hoodies, but that doesn't stop me feeling. I can't fool my brain into thinking they've gone away.

Something inside of me tells me to leave the bathroom, so I do. No real reason, I just feel like it. Or some bit of me feels like it. Whatever it is, I'm back in the cold corridor, feeling my way to my room. Goosebumps dance around on my arms and legs, popping up and down like the rats by the river going in and out of their little holes. That distracts the itching, for a few seconds. The image of the rats plays in my head: a dark evening, skinny tails, bead-eyes, up and down.

A distraction. I need a proper distraction. New goal.

~~Go to sleep.~~

~~Go to the bathroom.~~

Distract yourself.

What's distracting? My phone, but I'll never get to sleep staring at that electronic screen. If I stare long enough, I can sometimes see the individual pixels. I don't know if that's cool or worrying. Another option might be turning a light on and reading or doing that homework I really need to do. My brain and eyes protest at the mere thought.

Something which doesn't stress my eyes, or me, out. Right. Back at my bedroom door, I pull it open and nearly slip on the duvet which is still on the floor. I throw it back on the bed. For a moment, I consider following it, but then I spot a tiny bit of light creeping through the curtains. There are no streetlights directly outside the window. So...

Swaying over on unsteady feet, I hold onto the curtain for a moment before drawing it back. A quiet cul-de-sac stares up at me. Parked cars sit still, gathering a little frost. But my eyes look up, past everything sleeping on the ground.

The moon smiles at me. It glows, semi-covered by misty cloud.

There's my distraction. Nothing else matters when you look at the moon, right? It's like some sort of magical entity, existing in the sky for no real reason other than to comfort the lonely people who look up at it. Some god or goddess, maybe. Or a wheel of cheese. I don't care what it is—I just want to get lost in it.

It could be a tissue paper circle from a primary school kid's art project, cut around a plastic cup with safety scissors, and I would still love it.

There's nothing else that stares at you with such unwavering—

Itch.

No. As I was saying, there's—

Scratch.

The moon sighs.

Itch. Itch. Itch. Itch. Itch.

Grabbing the curtain, I fling it back across the rail, hiding the outside world. A growl nearly leaves my throat. I just want one night. One night! One night when I can sleep, or look at the moon, or do whatever I want to do. Why can't I have one night?

Itch itch itch itch itch itch itch itch—

I give up. Completely defeated, I flop onto my bed with balled fists, the alarm clock sneering at me. 12.11 AM. Time really chooses when to slow down. Detentions and waiting rooms and bad dysphoria nights.

I am Cyrus. I am Cyrus. I am Cyrus.

The words don't leave my lips, but a tear

dribbles down and wets them.

Advice

Gender dysphoria is a sense of unease that may be caused by a mismatch between someone's biological sex and their gender identity. This sense of unease or dissatisfaction may be so intense that it can have a harmful impact on daily life. (NHS, 2020)

Experiencing gender dysphoria is tough. While it can affect people to varying degrees, the experience is overwhelmingly negative and can be straight-up harmful. Of course, if you're experiencing gender dysphoria you should talk to someone—your parents or guardians, your therapist, your GP... anyone who might be able to help you. You may find ways of managing it yourself, which is great, but don't hesitate to reach out for help if you need it.

There are a few 'tricks' to try and make gender dysphoria a little less bad, such as distracting yourself. What's your favourite video game? Bet you can't play it for two hours straight. Just like that, you don't have to think about your gender dysphoria because you're wrapped up in the latest shoot-em-up from [Insert Cool Game Company Here]. Or painting amazing pictures, writing awesome stories... even homework (shudder) can be a distraction. You need to do your homework, by the way, stop procrastinating by reading!

Getting a referral to a gender clinic might be your ultimate goal, or it might not be. Hormone treatment and surgery might be your ultimate goals, but they also might not be. Everyone goes through things differently and gender dysphoria is no exception. If you just need to talk to someone for an hour every month, that's fine too. Binding or vocal training or even buying a new wardrobe might be all you want. But please, if you need help with your gender dysphoria—if it's getting worse or starting to affect your everyday life—reach out to someone you trust.

Resources

Websites

https://gids.nhs.uk/ - the Gender Identity Development Services website.
https://www.nhs.uk/conditions/gender-dysphoria/ - the NHS gender dysphoria website page.
https://www.counselling-directory.org.uk/gender-identity.html - gender identity help and advice.
https://mermaidsuk.org.uk/ - 19 and under trans, non-binary and gender-diverse charity.

Hotlines

020 8938 2030/1 - Gender Identity Development Services telephone number.
0808 801 0400 – Mermaids, transgender support for youth (19 and under), families and professionals.

Dad Jokes

Content Warnings

Censored Foul Language

DAD JOKES

Lily, she/her

"Goodnight, darling. Sleep well."

"Dad... can I talk to you for a sec?"

His hand pauses on the door frame, completely frozen. I gulp. It took a lot to say those words—days and days of planning and preparation, trying to figure out the right time, the right phrasing —but what am I meant to do now that they're out?

Worry moves his hand. Worry makes his face appear, round and disarmingly friendly, as his brain tries to figure out what's happening. I can guess a few of the options. Drugs. Pregnancy. Bullying. Disease. Well, maybe not disease—I'm only fourteen, it's not like I've got the guts to go to the doctor's on my own.

But everything else is up for grabs. The options thicken the air between us as he takes three tentative, dad-sized steps into my room, lowering himself onto my bed gradually. Like an old man. He's old to me, but I'm not so young that I think he's the oldest person in the world. I know the slowness means something else.

I hate this. I hate worrying him. I want to grab him by the shoulders and yell it all at once, but I can't. Forced to wait, I sit up and move a pillow to support my back, not quite meeting his eyes. This looks even worse. I'm ruining everything.

"What's on your mind, Lils?" There's confidence in his voice which doesn't dare to tremble. He has to appear strong—he has to be the dad, not the terrified teenager. But I know he wishes he could be anywhere else right now. No one wants to deal with their troublesome kid, they just want to show up to sports games and awards shows and congratulatory parents' evenings. They don't want complicated conversations at bedtime.

"I have something to tell you," *and I don't even know if you'll understand it, but I have to tell you otherwise my heart will burst*, "something really important. To me. I hope it's important to you too."

"... am I going to be a granddad?"

"Dad! I'm fourteen!"

Giggling a little, I take the moment to calm down. There are two options here: get it done with, or tread carefully and explore his knowledge first. The first choice is just ripping the plaster off, but it might make him confused. Confused people can lash out. Maybe not my dad, or at least the dad I know from all the time I've spent with him, but this... this can do weird things to people.

You want to know how someone really feels about you? Come out to them. Then you'll know.

Gripping the duvet with one of my hands, I reach over and hold his large fingers with the other. Hairs grow on them, thick and black. They accompany short, stubby fingernails that never grow over the ends of his fingers. Dirt has found its way beneath them, somehow. Mum'll get at him for that when he goes back to her. When I release him. Is that what this is? Some sort of social imprisonment?

He can leave if he wants to. He knows that.

But he won't, because I'm his daughter and he's my dad, so we're stuck here in my bedroom while darkness reigns outside and Mum has a bath. It sounds like a bath, anyway. Some sort of water. She could just be taking handwashing really seriously. Or a shower, but that's less fun than thinking she might've turned into Lady Macbeth.

High school really is taking over my brain.

"I'm not pregnant," I reiterate, just in case my outburst wasn't clear enough, "and I'm not sick. I'm not drinking or smoking or doing drugs."

"That's... that's everything I thought of," he sheepishly admits, counting down each idea on the fingers of his free hand, until all that's left is a harmless fist, "so it's nothing life-changing, then?"

"Maybe—sort of—I mean—" this isn't going great. It's not the absolute worst-case scenario, but it's definitely not the best either. "Dad, I'm asexual. And aromantic."

I can barely believe I just said those words. Relief courses through my veins, pulsing and rushing into every part of my body. For a moment, I'm not in my room. I'm somewhere else. Anywhere else. A cloud. A desolate mountain top. A planet with tiny green aliens. My fingers are dipping into stardust, golden and silver and shiny. It's getting everywhere, just like glitter. A sun shines down, then another. A field with grass so green it seems juicy, bursting with energy. An apple falls onto my head. I pick it up and see my face.

Then I'm back, and Dad is grinning.

"Hello 'asexual and aromantic', I'm Dad."

Silence. A long moment where I'm trying to figure out if he really just said that. Yeah. He just went there. Humour is a great way to break the ice, I guess, and at least we're away from the pregnancy questions, but... I'm still in shock. Seriously. A dad joke. Right now. Typical Dad, I guess.

"By the way, I have no idea what you just said."

There's still a wide smile on his face. There's something in it, understanding and sympathy and perplexment and all sorts of different things which turn into that smile. Unassuming. Waiting. Wanting to learn. Just wanting to see me happy, I guess. Everything the ideal parent should be.

It's not bad, me being asexual and aromantic, and I guess I technically don't have to tell anyone about it. It's personal. But I wanted to tell him. I've always been so open with him. He's... he's great. He really is.

I'm so lucky to have him as my dad.

"Asexual means I don't feel sexual attraction to people," saying 'sexual' to a parental figure feels weird, but I get through the ick and carry on, "and aromantic means I don't feel romantic attraction to people."

"Medical?"

"Not really."

"Bad?"

"Definitely not."

"Makes you happy?"

"Sort of? It's just who I am."

"That's like being an Ashwood supporter, that," he shakes his head, a mock-frown turning his lips downwards, "great one week and rubbish the next. Just who I am, right? Like who you are?"

"... sure, Dad, sure." I'm not going to tell him how angry the internet would be at him comparing sexualities to football teams. Instead, I nod and squeeze his hand, thankful for any little glimmer of understanding. "So... you're fine with it?"

"No babies, right?"

"Dad. I'm fourteen."

"Just checking!" He chuckles, pulling me into a bear hug which brings me way too close to the scent of sweat and weird aftershave. I feel bad for Mum sometimes.

But I love him, and I wrap my arms around his back to try and show that nothing has changed. There's a lot less weight on my shoulders now, but that's about it. Nothing else. I'm playing with the word 'life-changing' on my tongue, rolling it around and wondering. It depends on how you use it, but maybe my coming out is life-changing, and maybe it isn't. Technically, my life is now changed, just the same as my life would be changed if I was hit by a car tomorrow or if I bought a blue pen instead of a red one.

Life-changing is such a vast word.

It's changed my dad's life, a little bit. He was worried, and now he's not. Although he'll joke around whether he's worried or not, I know there's genuineness behind his smile. It's not negatively life-changing, but it's also not a lucky night at a talent show which skyrockets me into super-stardom. It's just a little thing.

I'm sort of lucky, really. There's no 'bringing the partner home' bit to coming out with me. Just me and my school bag walking through the front door every day. I guess that's something. It has taken me months to work out what was going on for years—all my friends getting crushes and 'boyfriends' that lasted for a few weeks if they even lasted to the end of the day. Meanwhile, I never felt anything. Still don't.

But I'm completely at peace with that, and myself.

"You know, I'm really glad it's not drugs," he says, pulling back from the hug and looking at me semi-seriously, "because drug dealers are some bad nuts. I bought shoes from one once; I ended up tripping everywhere!"

"Dad!" Face-palming, I can only shake my head and sigh. That's a barely related dad joke, the worst sort. Somehow, they're now popping up in my mind like wild beasts in a nature documentary. There's the large herd of general dad jokes, then the pairs of specific dad jokes. Lurking in the bushes is a rare dad joke, the 'almost good' one which pounces out of nowhere and disappears just as quickly.

If I'm not careful, he's going to make me insane. Hopefully not today, though, because I'm too happy to be insane today. Everything went okay. As okay as I can expect, I guess—there's no rainbow carpet being rolled out for me, no rainbow cake (I can't bake to save my life, as my burnt muffins from Year 7 can attest) and no celebrity appearances, but this is real life. This is my life, and I'm happy with how it went. Content. I can already see myself having the best night's sleep I've ever had, with nothing to worry me.

Except for that test next week.

Oh, and the homework due in on Wednesday.

Is my uniform out of the wash?

Never mind. Seems like I've got plenty to worry about, but not this anymore. No more 'coming out worries' for me! Well... I still have to tell Mum. I guess I could tell my brother, but he'll probably be too busy gluing his eyes to his games console to notice. My friends already know—the good ones, at least—and it doesn't really concern anyone else. Teachers don't need to know. Aunties and uncles can figure it out after a few years, or just keep on asking about a boyfriend. 'Or a girlfriend', they say, trying to make out that it's never a second, extra option, even though it always is. Boyfriend questions always come first.

Girlfriend questions start later when everyone's had too much to drink at family gatherings.

"I'll tell Mum if you want me to," he smiles again, and I start to suspect some sort of joke is coming out, but, in all seriousness, it'll be such a relief if he can do that, "and your brother. At some point. I never see him—does he still live here?"

"I'm surprised you can't hear him swearing all the time," I comment cheekily, testing the waters. Are we cool? His laugh tells me we're cool. My heart stops beating quite so fast. Not completely, though. That would be an entirely different but still pretty terrible problem.

As if on cue, a bold, lone expletive attacks my wall from the other side: the joys of having a bedroom directly next to your brother's. Not long after, there's a tiny beep. I know these noises so well that they're practically my personal night-time symphony. The games console has been turned on, which means the gaming must begin. Will it be until 2 AM or 3 AM? Maybe he'll go for a record and stay up until 5 AM. That would be impressive, but I'd rather not feel like I'm sleeping next to a warzone for the next eight hours.

There's some thought going on within Dad's forehead, some sort of weighing up. Pros and cons of telling my brother off, I bet. I don't really blame them, him and my mum, for mostly giving up on the gaming issue, though. He gets up on time and gets passing grades. The only problem is that he somehow manages to function on minus eight hours of sleep.

I'm assuming that staring at all those bright pixels subtracts sleeping hours, but don't quote me on that brilliant science.

"I will always love you and support you," Dad starts, but now I'm not sure whether it's because I just came out or because he wants me to do something, "but if you ever find a way to shut your brother up and get him to sleep on time, I will double your pocket money."

"What's that got to do with love?" Sitting here confused, I tilt my head to the side as a familiar theme tune, a little muffled by the wall, starts up. Is it bad that I recognise the music but have no idea what the game actually is? "And trust me, if I could stop him being a normal teenage boy, I would."

"That's my girl," patting me on the head, he starts to get off the bed, groaning and grunting for good measure before springing up and waving his hand in a mini bow. He's... he's definitely a character, that's for sure. "Oh, should I tell the cat as well?"

"... the cat has a name. She is called Tinkerbell." I point out, heavily emphasising her name in the hopes that one day he'll stop exclusively calling her 'the cat'. Too young to notice these things when we first got her, it took me years to stop also calling her 'the cat', after I realised her name was actually 'Tinkerbell'—and I named her in the first place. The shame haunts me to this day.

"I'll let you tell the cat. Goodnight, asexual and aromantic!"

Before I can protest, he's out of the room, shutting the door carefully like he always does. The click is almost comforting just due to its familiarity. My brother's endless noise, however, is less comforting, despite its frequency. Hearing my dad pop his head in his door and ask for the volume to be turned down is great.

He won't turn the volume down, but it's a nice gesture nonetheless.

Well... I survived. Nervousness and butterflies and sweaty hands have nothing on me. Not even Dad's dad jokes could discourage me. I told myself this morning that I'd come out to him today, him first out of everyone living under this roof. If he took it badly... I don't know what I would have done. But he didn't! That is a very important thing I must remember.

"DIE! EVIL SCUM! YOU ******* ****** ************! ****! I DIED!"

The other very important thing is to search for ways to cure my brother of his video gaming addiction. The internet must have answers. It always has answers; their frequency isn't the problem, just their trustworthiness. Maybe transferring him onto some nicer game might work. A farming simulator, or a puppy makeover, or a driving game where you're constantly capped at 20 mph—

"I HATE YOU ALL! **** WHY DIDN'T YOU ******* REVIVE ME? STUPID *****!"

Actually, I'd feel too sorry for the NPCs. Nobody deserves to listen to his half-baked abuse. Cold turkey is probably the best option for him.

But that's a struggle for another day. Right now, I need to roll over and scroll on my phone for hours and go to sleep.

Huh? What was that bit in the middle?

Nothing.

Goodnight, asexual and aromantic.

Advice

24% of LGBT people are not open to family members who they live with (excluding partners) about being LGBT. (GOV, 2017)

Coming out to your parents can be one of the scariest things that most of us ever do. For the vast majority of people, their opinions on LGBT+ people are either quiet or kept hidden, so coming out to people close to you can be something of a mystery. On top of that, sometimes parents are fine with other LGBT+ people, but their own child being LGBT+ can come as a shock.

That's an important aspect of coming out to the people you live with. Their initial reaction may not linger forever—if they seem to be in denial or confused, you may be able to explain your identity to them and educate them, or even just wait for it to sink in. Time is everything. Timing helps too, obviously; coming out just after a family tragedy or in the middle of a stressful event might not be the best option.

Hopefully, if you choose to come out to your parents or guardians, the experience is positive—or neutral at worst. But, just in case there's an extremely negative reaction, be prepared. Make sure you have somewhere safe to go and people you trust to turn to. If this isn't an option, there's hotlines and charities you can contact (below) who can help you out. Make sure you assess your situation before coming out—if it's not the right time, or if you already know your parents are anti-LGBT+, then think about your safety as a young person. If in doubt, wait a little longer—there's no rush to come out.

Resources

Websites

https://www.childline.org.uk/ - Childline website. http://lgbt.foundation/how-we-can-help-you - LGBT Foundation Website, providing a wide range of services to support lesbian, gay, bisexual and trans people.

Hotlines

0800 1111 – Childline hotline.
0345 3 30 30 30 – LGBT Foundation, advice, support and information.

Three Years

Three Years first appeared in Star Gazette Magazine

Content Warnings

Gender Clinic Waiting Lists
Non-Violent Intrusive Thoughts
Arguments

THREE YEARS

Jessica, she/her

Three years.

Leaning down, I clipped Sunshine's lead to his collar. He was a skinny thing, meant for running—Greyhound, or Greyhound mix, or something like that—probably more suited to a track than our tiny back garden. At least he had the fields, I guess. Every day, I'd clip that lead on and we'd walk right out of the cobweb-covered garage, down the alleyway behind the house and then... freedom.

Freedom was long grass which led to shady trees, a metal fence surrounding a horse racing track and then, beyond? The fields. Acres and acres of swaying corn, wheat, whatever the farmer chose that season. Sometimes grown, sometimes green. The little shoots pushing their heads up through tire-ruts and footprints were inspirational. The older plants, heads bowed, made you think.

Life, they seemed to whisper, *life has been and gone and will come again; won't you think about that for a while?*

We left the garage without any fuss. Between the ages of eleven and fifteen, I would call out to my mum every time I left with Sunshine. 'I'm leaving!', or 'Goodbye!', or 'See you later!'. The habit died off at around sixteen. Now eighteen, with a job and 'rent' and a university course, the words hadn't left my lips for a while. Not in that specific situation, anyway.

Three long years.

Other things had happened since then, as

well. Life was never easy. It always had some spanners to throw in the works: failed tests, breakups, discovering I was trans—oh, did I accidentally mention that last one? It snuck up on me, so I guess it's only fair it sneaks up on you too.

Sunshine didn't know I was trans. At least, I didn't think he did. He sniffed me just the same as he did when I was five and he was brought home, barely as big as a bean. Or so it seemed at the time —I think he was a bit bigger if I'm being honest. I'd put him on a cushion and stroke his tiny back at least once a day, after he tired himself out with all his playing and exploring. Every silver-grey hair needed to be smoothed down.

His hair was rougher than it used to be, as I took him down the alleyway. He had this peculiar thing where he'd only step directly on a cobble, meaning he looked a bit like a weird dressage horse when he went down the alleyway. Only the alleyway. As soon as we got to the grassy path, he relaxed into a normal walk, just by my ankle.

It's going to take three years.

Remembering the important part of the walk which I had fatally forgotten, I thrust my hand into my jacket pocket and pulled out some black earphones, already connected to a tiny iPod. Definitely not the newest, but not the oldest either. One of the little square ones. I forgot what it was called half of the time and forgot that it existed for the rest of it. Some music, whatever sort you want to think that it was, blasted in my ears. I winced.

I think Sunshine winced too. Sensitive dog ears and all that.

For whatever reason, music didn't seem so loud after a few hours, so I'd turn it up but then forget all about it when I turned the iPod off. Crazy, right? Some things just managed to slip through my mind like... like something slippery. Eels, maybe. I'd never seen an eel in real life. Did they even exist? Probably.

Such strange thoughts were common on dog walks, but they usually only happened once I passed through the treeline.

What was different about today?

Three years.

Oh. Maybe it was that. I stopped Sunshine at the end of the path, kneeling by his side to unclip the lead. Terraced houses looked onto the grass from a right angle. Little paths ran around the grass, random and mismatched, with bins placed just as randomly at some points. They sat where grass met road, or where path met path, or by that bench which was always just too wet to sit on (morning dew, I thought, was the culprit, added to a constant drizzle of rain on most days).

Sunshine ran. He always did. He knew the way better than I ever could, nosing around every weed and stone as if their minimal changes from day-to-day would drastically affect him. He trotted, loped and walked when it suited him, living without a care in the world. Just living, like the crops and the sun and the wind. I always seemed to get philosophical when there was no one around to listen.

Maybe that was for the best. Philosophy was a good way to lose friends.

Not that I had many of those.

Most disappeared after high school. Some disappeared even earlier, when I came out. Year 9. That was a wild year. College drove off the rest of them, as new people found new opinions on me, my identity and whatever I chose to wear. Skirts, and I was trying too hard. Pants, and I was faking it. Makeup, and I looked 'like a drag queen'. None, and I looked like a boy.

Nothing worked, so I stopped trying to appease everyone else and simply did what felt best.

That was usually whatever made me feel the most feminine, so skirts and makeup were my go-to. On lazy days, tracksuits with my hair streaming down my chest. It always helped. The hair, I mean. I was lucky that it grew so much—my mum said I got her genes for that, the long, straight black locks that she braided so intricately down her back. I never bothered, but I could do it. She taught me.

That was a good day. Some tears at the end, some close hugs that felt like they lasted for hours. But it was a good day.

I'm sorry, Jessica, but it's three years.

Jessica. Jess-i-ca. My mum chose it. I keep going on about her, but it's true. I guess she's been the one person I could rely on, always. There's never a day without a meal on the table, or a funny story about Grandma, or... well, whatever other domestic niceties you can think of. You do the work. I was busy.

I was meant to be walking Sunshine, but my mind seemed to be walking itself. It always happened. Music didn't help. To be fair, I think silence was worse. There was me, going off on random thought trails again. Nothing made sense. Everything flip-flopped. Sunshine flopped onto the ground when he saw a dog bigger than him. It was a... uh... I was never very good with dog breeds. But we were almost at the trees, so nothing mattered.

Under those leaves, the rest of the world melted away. Even that big dog.

Maybe it was a Labrador. They were common, so that guess had to have good odds.

We passed under the trees once Sunshine stopped being an idiot and flopping all over the place. He started racing through leaves and bushes, chasing poor squirrels who never did anything to him. I stuck to the path, like always. I must have seemed boring to him. He pranced around while my mind spun and pondered until it hurt.

Why was being alive so difficult?

The trees had it right. They just stood and grew, sometimes spinning, sometimes not. Their leaves fell, sure, but they grew back. Like forever returning children, if children became babies every time they came home. That made no sense, but it did.

Waiting for three years.

In three years, I would have a new job. New home. New partner, maybe. Qualifications and whatever else university brought. New friends. Perhaps a new pet.

Apparently, I would also have my first gender clinic appointment in three years.

Patients who were referred in 2017 were only just being seen in 2020. Three years. Long, long, long years. I was a patient who was referred in 2020, so where did that leave me? Waiting, obviously. Eternally.

Sunshine barked. Another squirrel. Grey. Those were the invaders, weren't they? From Europe. Or America. No, they'd never swim all the way from America. But did they swim the Channel? Maybe I should've taken Geography at GCSE.

Did I take Geography?

No, no. I took History.

My memory was worrying sometimes. Only sometimes, but it was enough to be noticeable. Semi-noticeable. What was I even thinking? The fence was approaching, and I was stuck in a black hole of wondering about squirrels, GCSEs and memory, which all somehow fitted together. It was a maddening jigsaw. Luckily, I didn't think about it for too long.

I never seemed to think about anything for too long. Until I did.

This must really be confusing you.

Three years is ridiculous, Jessica, I'm so sorry.

Mum. When the fence came into view, that meant we turned directly left. That led to the fields.

Mum always supported me the most. She never got mad, or sad, or anything else that rhymes with those two words. She complained about the things I complained about and loved the things I loved. She took me shopping for skirts and crop tops and whatever else she could think of. Turning down glittery hair bows and earrings which belonged on five-year-olds was difficult, but I managed it with a smile. She brushed my hair and told me exactly which shampoos and conditioners to use as it grew, and grew, and grew.

In three years, my hair would be down to my ankles. She said that. It would be trailing on the floor, she said, it'd be so long I'd be stepping on it. Tripping over it.

Sunshine shot off after a bird. Some sort of pigeon. Its wings flapped, panicked, as it escaped to the safety of a tree. Luckily for it, Sunshine couldn't climb. He tried. Jumped up at the trunk, ripping it with his claws. Only a little, but he'd left his mark on the world. The evidence was staring me in the face for the few seconds I spent looking at it, still walking past. I didn't pause.

I wanted to get to the fields.

Music accompanied me down the path. Sunshine sort of did too, but his constant rushing about made the effect a little underwhelming. It was funny, sometimes, when he'd race away but other slower dogs would walk by my heels and roll onto their stomachs for tickles in the middle of the path. It sounds odd, but it happened quite a lot.

There was a metal gate at the very end of the path, connected to the fence. The fence turned right and ran around the horse racing track, giving a wide berth for the various paths which led to the fields. I could see them as we approached it. Green ground. Newly planted crops, but not so new that you couldn't see them yet. Just young.

Was I young? That depended on who you asked. My mum would swear I was young until the day I died, but all my friends—the ones who stayed—said I was 'mature', whatever that meant. The makeup helped, I reckoned, on the days when I could be bothered. Or maybe my voice. I hated it, but deeper voices usually meant people were older.

I would have given anything to have the squeaky, ear-piercing voice of a Year 7.

Well.

Maybe not a Year 7. Year 8, though, definitely. *Three. Years.*

Tiny, budding crops roamed across the fields, acting like a horizon. They spread out so far that you could only see them and the sky, meeting in a grey-green embrace. Of course, I couldn't have a sunny day—whatever was controlling the sky simply wouldn't allow it. But a light breeze accompanied the shadiness of the clouds so neatly that I could barely wish for tropical weather. I always complained about the heat, anyway.

Why do I have to wait three years to be

myself?

That was a mystery greater than any I could ever come up with. Sunshine barked. He found a pheasant in the field.

I smiled. Waiting lists shoved aside, I filled my head with the freshness of the air and thought of blissful nothing.

Advice

The NHS Gender Identity Clinic currently has a waiting list of 33 to 36 months, which is 2.75 to 3 years. (GIC, 2020)

Being on any sort of waiting list isn't great, but when it's a waiting list for one of your only options for medically transitioning without great cost, it's considerably worse. The only real possible advice here is don't put off being referred if you don't have any reason to (don't procrastinate) and make sure you have a support system of any sort in place for your wait. For many people, it's not a great feeling.

It might seem like gender dysphoria worsens while you wait, since you're 'not doing anything'. I tactfully refer to this as 'limbo'. Try to remember that this isn't your fault, and the waiting list isn't going to magically get shorter if you get really sad about it. At least, that hasn't worked for me, and I've complained about it a lot. Continue to seek support from wherever you usually receive it and look into non-medical options for relieving gender dysphoria if you experience it.

Some of these options might be learning how to use makeup (if you manage it, I commend you—that takes *skill*), chest-binding, tucking, packing and any other method of affirming your true gender. Even keeping friends and family around you who use your preferred name and pronouns can help. It can feel like there's no hope, and that three years is an immensely long time, but the time *will* pass. I promise.

Resources

Websites

https://gids.nhs.uk/ - the Gender Identity
Development Services website.
https://www.nhs.uk/oneyou/every-mind-matters -
NHS youth mental health support.
https://youngminds.org.uk/find-help/ - youth mental
health support.
https://www.east-ayrshire.gov.uk/Resources/PDF/L/
LGBT-Guide-for-Young-Transgender-People.pdf -
NHS guide on many aspects of young trans life.
https://mermaidsuk.org.uk/ - 19 and under trans, non-
binary and gender-diverse charity.

Hotlines

020 8938 2030/1 - GIDS telephone number.
0808 801 0400 – Mermaids youth (19 and under),
families and professionals transgender support
hotline.

Never Serious

Content Warnings

Mention Of Sex
Mention Of Sex-Related Drugs
Mild Argument

Callum, he/him

ROB
U up?

> **CALLUM**
> you shouldn't be. school tomorrow.

ROB
Not my fault I can't sleep

> **CALLUM**
> might be. all those energy drinks.

ROB
Shut up, you drink them too.

> **CALLUM**
> and we're both up, so i'm right. :p

ROB
I didn't text u for a weird argument about energy drinks, u know.

> **CALLUM**
> figured that out when you first text me. so, who's sending pics first?

ROB
BABE!

CALLUM

wut?

ROB

Did not mean that.

CALLUM

oh. sorry. so what do you want?

ROB

Charming.

CALLUM

it's 3am, this is all i got. you get charm when it's normal hours and i'm not half asleep.

ROB

I'm worried, babe.

CALLUM

you dying?

ROB

Probably, but it's not that.

CALLUM

so...

ROB

It's awkward.

CALLUM
erectile dysfunction?

ROB
BABE

CALLUM
it's oki, i know someone who sells viagra at school

ROB
It's. Not. That.

CALLUM
oh. so what is it?

ROB
I've been thinking.

CALLUM
dangerous.

ROB
Cliche.

CALLUM
touche. carry on.

ROB
So.

CALLUM

when i said carry on i sorta meant actually carry on.

ROB

Babe, I love you but I also want to murder you.

CALLUM

trust me, feeling's mutual. you woke me up at 3am.

ROB

I thought you were already awake?

CALLUM

that detail is meaningless. carry on.

ROB

Anyway, I was thinking about how we can never be proper, u know?

CALLUM

...wut? i thought your mum was chill with us??

ROB

Not like that, and she is. She asked if u liked the meal she cooked, actually, but I forgot to ask u. Did u like it?

CALLUM

yeah yeah it was great, her cooking's awesome, but go back to the last part

ROB
The meal?

                                   CALLUM
stop playing dumb, idiot. wdym we can't be proper?

ROB
U know what I mean. Don't make me go into it.

                                   CALLUM
dumb babe, i have NO idea what you mean.

ROB
Don't call me dumb babe, that's mean.

                                   CALLUM
you woke me up at 3am just to confuse me!!! THAT
is mean!!!!! also i love u but u are confusing the heck
out of me

ROB
I'm sorry. I'm tired. And sad.

                                   CALLUM
just tell me what you mean by 'not proper', explain it
like i'm an idiot (like u)

ROB
This is text. U can't whisper in text.

CALLUM

just did. tell me what you mean anyway.

ROB

Well, we're both guys.

CALLUM

yes. that's sorta required for being boyfriends.

ROB

So we can't ever be proper. Or serious.

CALLUM

...tell me, very, very slowly, what you mean by 'proper' and 'serious'.

ROB

U know. Like mum and dad. Or your dad and Miss Liss.

CALLUM

she hates being called that. it's just liss and u know it. but i still don't get what you mean?

ROB

Married. That's what I mean. We can't get married.

CALLUM

...
Robert.
You are an idiot.

Who lives under a rock.

ROB
Huh?

CALLUM
just to make sure, why don't you think we can get married?

ROB
It's the law, right?

CALLUM
jeez. google is free, you know? maybe try it out one day?

ROB
What are u saying?

CALLUM
we can get married, dumb babe. civil partnership or normal marriage or whatever u want. next u gonna be saying gay sex is illegal.
before u say anything, yes we're technically old enough to have sex but no i am not having sex with you yet

ROB
I feel stupid. I'm sorry for waking u up.

CALLUM

it's oki. i'll always wake up for you, dumb babe.

ROB

Please don't call me that in public, ever.

CALLUM

no promises.

ROB

Babe?

CALLUM

ya?

ROB

Will you marry me?

CALLUM

no, u idiot.

ROB

What? Why?

CALLUM

coz we're 16. ask me again in like 3 years. maybe 4. i love u.

ROB

I love you too. You wanna sleep?

CALLUM
i've wanted to sleep since 9. but ya. see u tomorrow.

ROB
Love you.

CALLUM
love you too. get sleep.

ROB
Will do.
Out of curiosity, who sells viagra at school?

CALLUM
babe. go to sleep.

Advice

Three in five LGBT students have never been taught that same-sex couples can get married and have civil partnerships. (Stonewall, 2017)

You should (keyword here being 'should') be taught about same sex marriage and civil partnerships at school, but there's always a chance that you won't be, for whatever reason. Great, the place that's meant to teach you isn't teaching you what you actually need—anyone surprised?

Okay, I'll get serious. No more digs at the education system (which is hopefully improving). If you are in a same-sex relationship, you can get married (even religiously, in some religious institutions—not all of them, but some), or you can get a civil partnership. Yeah, you might've been thinking that we can only get civil partnerships; I'll be honest, I thought that too. But you can get legally married to a same-sex partner if you want to!

This is obviously a great thing for those of us who want to get married, or get civil partnerships, but what isn't great is the lack of knowledge around it. There are some places below where you can read up about it, in case your school doesn't cover it (or doesn't cover it properly/extensively enough for anyone to understand what they're trying to say). Oh, and please don't wake up your partner at 3 AM because of a misunderstanding about it—just a pro tip for you.

Resources

Websites

https://www.gov.uk/marriages-civil-partnerships - England and Wales marriage and civil partnership information.
https://www.mygov.scot/births-deaths-marriages/marriage-civil-partnerships/ - Scotland marriage and civil partnership information.
https://www.nidirect.gov.uk/information-and-services/government-citizens-and-rights/births-deaths-marriages-and-civil-partnerships - Northern Ireland marriage and civil partnership information.

Wrong
Group Chat

Content Warnings

Racism (Exclusion Because Of Race)
Racial Prejudices
Foul Language
Mention Of Transphobia
Arguments

Rose, she/her

xXemlovescakeXx
xXemlovescakeXx has invited you to: PRE PRIDE
PARTY WOO YAY

lovehearts_rosepetals
u idiot
this is the wrong group chat

a-person-who-exists
Wdym wrong group chat?
Is there another group chat? I was never invited to
one??

lovehearts_rosepetals
thanks a lot, emma, you're a complete idiot

tiredandgay.com
maybe you should be nicer to your girlfriend?

lovehearts_rosepetals
ugh shut up.
look, there is another group chat, but it's got a very
good reason for existing
and for u not being part of it

sxphxe
Yeah, it's because you all suck.

lovehearts_rosepetals
not exactly

a-person-who-exists
Not exactly???
So kind of???

sxphxe
I thought asians were meant to know everything,
stop asking so many dumb questions

xXemlovescakeXx
sophiee
u can't say that
melia?

lovehearts_rosepetals
she can say whatever she wants, especially if it's
'emma is an idiot'
why do i have to sort everything out anyway?

a-person-who-exists
You used to be nice.
And I'm not even responding to that Sophie, nice try
to get a rise out of me tho.

sxphxe
Just spitting facts over here, don't mind me.

xXemlovescakeXx
melia??

lovehearts_rosepetals
why don't you ask someone who gives one, emma?

a-person-who-exists
Great, you don't care about someone being racist to your friend.

sxphxe
Not racist if it's true.

tiredandgay.com
Shut the fuck up.

sxphxe
Ooh, gayboy getting spicy.

tiredandgay.com
Wtf does that even mean?

callmewhateveruwant
um, sophie?

sxphxe
LOL I didn't think you were still in this group chat
Wassup Ava?

a-person-who-exists
How can you just talk normally after all the shit you've been saying?

sxphxe
Man I hope your parents don't find your phone, using a swear word, ooh

a-person-who-exists
I swear to God Sophie
If you hate me just say it don't be a fucking asshole, you've had 2 years to tell me

sxphxe
Now you're being rude and interrupting Ava. Guess you're not little miss perfect after all

a-person-who-exists
I'm this close to punching you

callmewhateveruwant
uh it's fine i was just gonna say
if everyone's sorta not too busy

tiredandgay.com
Sophie's busy being racist and Amelia's busy not caring about it so I think you're fine

callmewhateveruwant
well um it was sorta about the whole 'gayboy' thing it's just something happened today and i think maybe that's why that word was used and yknow like it shouldn't have been used but maybe i know why?

callmewhateveruwant has been removed from the group chat

lovehearts_rosepetals
now i'm curious what happened?

sxphxe
Nothing.
Assholes being assholes.
Outside the toilets again.
But I'm not fucking talking about it.

a-person-who-exists
Sophie, you literally experience so much transphobia at school and it breaks my heart but casual racism is somehow fine?

lovehearts_rosepetals
stop calling it racism

a-person-who-exists
IT IS RACISM

sxphxe
I really don't care any more, the only reason we didn't invite you to Emma's stupid little pre pride party is because your parents won't let you go anyway, because you're asian

a-person-who-exists
That literally means nothing
My parents are coming with me to pride?

lovehearts_rosepetals
look, we didn't invite ethan either, but he's not
bothered
AND he's not chinese so it's not racist coz it's not just
u

a-person-who-exists
I'M NOT FUCKING CHINESE
I've known you since Year 7, you've met my fucking
parents and you KNOW we're Taiwanese. But that
shouldn't even matter anyway.
I'm done. I don't give a shit. You're all shit friends and
I don't need this shit.

sxphxe
I was gonna make a 'language' joke but that's too
easy.

tiredandgay.com
Stop being a piece of shit Sophie.

sxphxe
ugh

*tiredandgay.com has been removed from the group
chat*

xXemlovescakeXx
i'm sorta not comfortable with this guys you're being

kinda mean

a-person-who-exists
YOU'RE not comfortable?
And kinda? Wtf Emma.

lovehearts_rosepetals
just shut up emma

a-person-who-exists
Stop being a dick to your girlfriend and stop being a fucking racist

xXemlovescakeXx
i can make a new group chat? with everyone in?

lovehearts_rosepetals
what the why do you think that's a good idea god you're dumb
all the snowflakes hate us now, why would they want to be in a new group chat with us?

xXemlovescakeXx
idk i just
don't want anyone to fall out with each other

a-person-who-exists
Bit late for that.
Have fun at your pre pride party, I'll just go to ACTUAL pride with ACTUAL friends.

sxphxe
Good luck finding any.

lovehearts_rosepetals
can we all just like calm down
literally all this drama over nothing i stg

a-person-who-exists

And that's exactly why I'm leaving. Have a nice life.

a-person-who-exists has left the group chat

Advice

51% of Black, Asian and minority ethnic LGBT people have experienced discrimination or poor treatment from others in their local LGBT community because of their ethnicity. (Stonewall, 2016)

Racism should not be tolerated within LGBT+ communities and spaces, or anywhere else, but, somehow, it manages to leak through. It really is illogical. Both communities are oppressed and have been historically hated and discriminated against, and both still face discrimination today. So, why is there racism in the LGBT+ community?

Well, people can be gay and racist, to put it simply. Just the same as someone could be Black and homophobic, being a part of one of the two communities doesn't mean that people automatically like, respect or even tolerate the other. It's a shame, but it is the reality we are facing. You can help to change this, though.

In high school and college, you might hear a lot of 'casual racism'—snide, hateful comments about or relating to someone's race. Call. Them. Out. It's not acceptable, but a lot of teenagers think it is because no one ever challenges it. Similarly, if you notice your friends quietly excluding another friend due to their race, stop them and confront them about it. Lots of racism is subtle (although overt racism still exists and is a terrible problem) but that means that it just takes a little confidence to call it out and stamp it out.

Resources

Websites

 https://www.stonewall.org.uk/bame-and-poc-lgbt-communities - information on BAME and POC LGBT+ communities.
https://www.stonewallscotland.org.uk/about-us/news/qtipoc-organisations-you-should-know-about - QTIPOC (Queer, Trans, Intersex People Of Colour) organisations.
https://www.manchesterpride.com/blog/queer-black-bame-and-poc-charities-organisations-and-community-groups - Queer Black, BAME and POC charities, organisations and community groups.

The Rules

Content Warnings

Mention Of Gender Dysphoria
Mention Of Unsupportive Parents
Mention Of Unsafe Binding
Tobacco Use

THE RULES

J, he/him

Daniel was an angel against the bustling backdrop of the park. An angel dressed in a dark hoodie and ripped jeans (just like every time I saw him outside of school) with dreads falling down his back, uncontrolled and beautiful. *Handsome*, I mentally corrected myself. He hated the word 'beautiful'; it was because of something about his mum that he didn't want to get into. He was a handsome angel.

Clasping my hands together, I crossed my legs and waited for him to get closer. Then uncrossed them. Crossing your legs was girly, wasn't it? Or was it the other way round? I knew one of them was bad, but I could never remember which one.

Manspreading. I could do that, considering I was the only person sitting on the bench, and I knew that was masculine. It was sort of in the name. *Man*spreading.

Feeling confident, I began to manspread.

"Jesus, I get over here and you suddenly take up the whole bench; what you tryna say?" he laughed, slinging his bag off his shoulder and letting it fall to the ground. I flinched at the thump it made, knowing what was in there. "Don't worry, J, it ain't made of glass. Or I hope it ain't, anyway."

"I know, I know," cheeks turning a little red, I stopped manspreading and shuffled up the bench to give him some space, tensing as his arm swooped around my shoulders. He froze.

"Sorry, J. I forgot," the arm disappeared, diving down to retrieve the bag instead, and I breathed out carefully, "but I can make it up to you, ay? It came in the post this morning."

Deep inside my chest, I became aware of my heart beating. Similarly, a pulse began throbbing in my neck. It was actually here. I hadn't dared to hope too much in the weeks leading up to its arrival, but if it had actually arrived? If it was actually in Daniel's bag? I could hope then, couldn't I?

No. No expectations. As soon as I got my hopes up, they were always dashed. It would be too small. Or too big. Or the wrong colour—but I could live with that. There'd be something wrong. There had to be. It would have holes, or it wouldn't work. The universe wouldn't allow me to have a completely happy day. It would disrupt something, and then everything would come crashing down. Cows would fall from the sky.

Or something. There had to be *something*.

"I didn't open it," the package he pulled out of his backpack was fairly small and rectangular, white and thin, "'cause I thought you might've wanted to do that, considering it's your first. Mum said congrats, by the way. Oh!" Putting the package down for a moment, he turned to me and looked into my eyes with a fierceness that would have surprised me, had I not known him for way too many years. "Mum said you can come over for tea today if you want. To celebrate, or something, but I think that's just her excuse for seeing you and fawning all over ya—she doesn't do that to me, you know! I'm her child!"

"She's really nice," I smiled, laughing a little at the mock-outrage on Daniel's face, "I'll ask my parents."

"Sweet. Anywho, open it!"

All of a sudden, the package was thrust onto my lap. My heart thumped in my throat—how did it get there? But my fingers wouldn't wait for that biological debate. They moved, considering the packaging and turning it over before delicately tearing at the papery material. I knew I couldn't damage the contents just by opening it, but some desperate part of me told me to be careful. Anything could go wrong. I was still due some sort of disaster for that day, and it could have appeared at any moment.

Inside, a plastic-wrapped binder met my disbelieving eyes. It was actually there. I could touch it. A full-length chest binder, which, when I unravelled the plastic and held it up with both hands, looked a lot like a tank top. Dark brown. Real. Perfect.

"Oh my God, I'm such an idiot!" As I nearly dropped the binder in shock, Daniel slapped his forehead and sighed deeply, confusing me, "I got it in the wrong colour!"

"I... didn't ask for a colour," I pointed out, but he groaned and waved his hand.

"I always get mine in skin colour, like nude or whatever you call it, but I forgot you're white!" I couldn't stop giggling as he made a show of slapping his forehead quite a few times. "Auto-pilot mode, you know, I just clicked and clicked and bam! Wrong colour. I'm so stupid, I'm sorry—"

"It's fine," tentatively, I placed my hand on his shoulder, trying to look into his eyes like he looked into mine—I failed, but I think he appreciated the effort; he stopped beating up his forehead, in any case, "brown is fine, no one will see it anyway. I don't do PE, not like you."

"I could never give up football," he shrugged, slouching back on the bench. "I got the size right, right? Small?"

"Yeah," the memory of trying to measure my chest in Daniel's bathroom, with him yelling random measurements and eventually just random words from outside the door, was a funny yet overwhelmingly unproductive one. We did work out my size, but it also took about an hour.

For a little while, our conversation fizzled out. I began people-watching, finding the skaters on the nearby ramps pretty interesting. My hands still touched the binder as if they were scared that it might have disappeared at any moment. For all I knew, it could have. Something had to go wrong. Something.

My parents wouldn't let me go to tea at Daniel's house, or they'd discover the binder and flip out. If they even knew what it was. They'd assume, anyway. Everything was suddenly because I was trans—arguments, missed questions on homework, forgetting to do some chores, snapping at my brother... the list went on. Even watching a new TV programme (which had absolutely nothing to do with anything LGBT+, considering it was a nature documentary) was considered a product of my very unsuccessful coming out as trans. It was hopeless.

So, if the binder didn't spontaneously combust, my parents would do something to ruin the day. They had to. The universe had to stay balanced, so a bad thing had to follow a good thing. I didn't make the rules. I just observed them and tried to stay on the good side of them.

"J, I do have to tell you some things, before you start wearing it," Daniel said, probably looking back into my eyes again—unfortunately, my vision consisted of the floor at that moment in time, so I couldn't quite tell, "there's some—well, have you seen those 'binding tip' posts on Instagram?"

"No," I replied honestly.

I didn't tell him the reason, but, in truth, my eyes welled up with tears every time I saw anything related to a trans masculine experience online. I couldn't have anything or do anything, and I wouldn't allow myself to get my hopes up, so all they did was make me miserable.

I stayed well away. It was getting to the point where I couldn't count the number of times I'd scrolled past a post just because it said 'trans' on it.

Out of context, that sounded quite transphobic, but I guess that's why context is important. My English teacher seemed to think it was, anyway.

"You just love making my life easy, don't ya?" He sighed, but I gingerly raised my eyes to check his face and found his usual grin. A little relief trickled through my system. "Right, well, there are some rules for binding, you know. 'The rules'," his air quotation marks made me smile and sit up a bit, nodding to encourage him to continue, "so that you don't mess up your body."

"I can mess up my body?" A small alarm bell started ringing in my mind. A doctor's appointment because of a 'messed up body' didn't sound like a good idea.

"You're not gonna mess it up, because you're gonna listen to the rules," he made to put his arm around me again, before thinking for a moment and putting it back down, "anyway, sorry, the rules. Yeah, there are a couple rules I have to tell you before you go anywhere near that binder."

"I'm already near it," I pointed out.

"That is true," he agreed, going silent for a moment. "Before you put it on, anyway."

A few tiny kids on bikes far too big for them chose that exact second to rush past, screaming something at each other. Someone had stolen a phone, it seemed. Or maybe a coat. Everything sounded the same when it was said in a high-pitched squeal.

Daniel waited for them to pass, so I took the opportunity to look down at the binder again. The dark brown fabric looked up at me. It didn't have an expression, but it was definitely looking. That could have been curiosity, I guessed, or wariness. There was no way of knowing, but my thoughts pondered over it for a second anyway.

The top half looked different to the bottom half. Not wanting to get my hopes up, I hadn't even looked at the website Daniel bought it from, and I'd never really seen one. Glimpses of Daniel's had been revealed to me through his shirt moving around and other little actions, but that only properly showed the colour. You couldn't tell what the shape of a piece of clothing was from a centimetre of material.

But now I had a chance to look at it properly, knowing it was mine—at least, for the time being. If my parents found it, it would likely become the property of the rubbish bin. But, moving past that miserable thought, I let one of my fingers trail down it. The bottom half was thin and light, while the top had a black inside and seemed firmer. The 'binding' bit, I guessed. That was what set it apart from being just a tank top.

It was also what made it cost £35, but that was neither here nor there.

Well, it kind of was. £35 was a *lot* of pocket money. Weeks of chores and spending absolutely nothing meant that my energy drink habit disappeared, which might have been a blessing in disguise, and Daniel tried to buy me things all the time. I'd gotten used to refusing them. In reality, no one needed that massive bag of crisps to eat while we hung out after school, or the copious amounts of neon green, purple and pink cans we bought.

Having something which I actually wanted to buy put a lot of other things into perspective. Handing over the £35 when Daniel first ordered it, a few weeks ago, felt not only celebratory but also remarkably *adult*. I had saved for something and bought it. Nothing revolutionary, I knew, but, to me, it was a little marker of freedom. Maturity. *Something*. Something other than the short-lasting sugar high off of 50p chocolate and £1 drinks.

Or 17p drinks if you went to the right supermarket.

"Stupid kids have great timing," with the 'stupid kids' gone, Daniel started again, "but, as I was saying, you need to bind safely. To not mess with your body, your ribs, all that. Following me so far?"

"Need to bind safely to protect body," I nodded.

"And the way you bind safely is by *listening* to your body," he continued, "following?"

"You've completely lost me," admitting that made Daniel roll his eyes, but I honestly had no idea what 'listening to your body' was unless it was something to do with your heartbeat. Or your pulse. Maybe blood pressure? I was well and truly lost.

"Okay, let me put it a different way," he was quiet for a few seconds, then shook his head, "nope, you know what? Let's just do the actual rules. They're easy to understand. You got a notebook?"

I did. It was a little beat up, since everything

which was made of paper that went in my bag got destroyed eventually, but it had only been in for a few weeks. That meant a few pages were crumpled and there was a coffee stain on the back cover, but it was usable.

If I remembered correctly, I was pretty sure that Daniel bought me it for my last birthday. Something to help me be less scatter-brained or something, not that I thought I was scatter-brained, but apparently he did. If anything, *I* thought that *he* was scatter-brained.

Despite all that, I pulled the notebook out and hunted for a pen. Pen found, I flicked to an empty page.

"Right. Rule number one," he waited as I scribbled down 'Rule number one' diligently, just like if I was in class taking notes (although I was a little more invested in these mysterious 'listening to your body' rules than Physics or Maths) "is to *never* sleep in your binder. Ever."

"No sleeping in binder," I parroted back to him, writing the words down next to 'Rule number one' in my note-taking scrawl. It was readable, but only by me. Teachers hated it.

"Rule number two," again, he paused, and again, I wrote down his words, "is never wear your binder for more than eight hours at a time. And take breaks within the eight hours, if you can."

"No more than eight hours, take breaks," in my head, I was trying to mentally calculate how long the school day was, but I couldn't think and write about different things so I ended up giving up and just getting the rule down on paper.

"Rule number three," pause, scribble, "is don't do heavy exercise in your binder. Or anything above mild, if you can help it. Which leads me to rule four —"

"Still writing, Daniel," I cut in, apologetic for interrupting him but also furiously writing down the last rule.

"Sorry."

He waited for me to catch up, as 'don't exercise in binder' got put down on the paper. I didn't actually exercise much anyway, especially since my high school decided that leaving me out of PE altogether was the best way to deal with a trans student who didn't complain about missing out on sports, but it would be important if I suddenly got hit on the head by a brick and became a gym nut.

"You ready?"

"Yeah, go ahead," eyes down on the paper and pen at the ready, I prepared for the next rule.

"Final rule, really—uh, what were we up to?"

"Rule number four," I helped him out.

"Yeah! Rule number four—if you feel any pain or discomfort in your chest, or you're struggling to breathe, or any other bad thing which might be your binder's fault, take it off immediately," I glanced up and found his serious eyes glaring down at me, sending a shiver up my arms, "and try and give it a rest for a day, maybe a couple. If it keeps on getting worse, go to the doctor."

"But the other rules mean that shouldn't happen, right?" Quickly writing down the last rule ('pain/discomfort/no breathing, take off binder, still bad, go to doctor'), I looked up again to ask the question, "they mean I won't mess up my body?"

"Should do the trick," he confirmed, a smile crossing onto his lips again, "just don't forget them. Oh, you can swim in that binder, if you want to, but I usually use an older one. Not that you have an older one yet, but just a tip for later on."

"Got it," I said.

Not writing that one down, I closed the notebook and put both it and the pen back in my bag. The bike kids had migrated to the skate park and were annoying the mainly teenage skaters. One of them was waving a lit cigarette around, seemingly to try and get them to move away, but it instead caused a crowd to appear around him, all chirpily asking for their own 'cigs' in nasal voices. Poor guy.

The park was crazy. It always was, considering it was only a few minutes away from both a high school and a primary school and was near the bus stop which all the college kids got off at. But, just on that day, the park contained a handsome angel who gave me an answer to relentless chest-related gender dysphoria.

I'd never been more thankful to have a friend as awesome as Daniel.

Advice

Don't wear a binder for long periods of time, or sleep in it. (GC2B, 2020)

Binding is a good way to relieve chest-related gender dysphoria—I should know, since I myself have a binder for that exact reason. But you can't ignore 'the rules', as Daniel puts it, of chest binding.

Make sure you purchase a binder from a reputable business (I recommend GC2B, as that's where I've gotten all of my binders) if you can and be wary of products without any reviews or ratings. Cheap options might be more accessible, but quality is quite important in ensuring your safety while binding, and it can be difficult to assess from looking at a product page on a phone screen. If you put on a binder and immediately feel pain, take it off. Binding is not meant to hurt you.

Taking regular breaks can help, especially if you're unable to fully take your binder off due to school hours. My advice? Go into a bathroom stall and remove your binder at lunch, or during breaks if you feel you need to. You can put it back on before you go outside, but it'll give your chest a break from binding. There's plenty of advice out there (see below) but, above all, listen to your body. Unlike what my Karate teacher once told me, if it's hurting, it's not working.

Resources

Websites

https://www.gc2b.co/ - sells binders.
https://www.underworks.com/ - sells binders.
https://pointofpride.org/chest-binder-donations/ -
donated binders for those in need.
http://point5cc.com/binding-101-tips-to-bind-your-
chest-safely/ - safe binding tips.

That's Not Their Name

Content Warnings

Deadnaming
Getting In Trouble At School
Arguments
Mention Of Tobacco Use
Mention Of Unsupportive Family

THAT'S NOT THEIR NAME

Emily, she/her

"Jenna?"

"Which one, miss?"

"Very funny. We've done this register all year, Jenna, you should know by now that you come first. Jenna Adams, please."

That joke had gotten old, I agreed with Mrs Pike on that one. Stuck in that boring Maths classroom—even the walls were boring, filled with equations and numbers stretched to look like smiley faces—I couldn't bring myself to roll my eyes. The register would have been the most boring part of the lesson, but this was Maths. Number-filled Hell.

Hell wouldn't be fiery or filled with demons and devils. It would be a plain white room with only a desk and a chair, and a Maths exam paper which never ended sat on the desk. That would be Hell.

"Matthew?"

"Here."

Taking the register was quite repetitive, though. I leaned back in my chair, snug in the back corner of the room, checking the backs of everyone's heads. I didn't care about most of them. Just that little blond in the front row, the tiny thing which I called my best friend. I meant it, like, but they were tiny. Even though we were in Year 9, they got mistaken for a Year 7 more times than I could count. Teachers would shove them out of the Year 9 lunch queue before they could get a word in edgeways. Life wasn't fair to everyone, but it really did a number on them.

This register was important to them. I knew that. I'd been there when we confronted Mrs Pike— no, not exactly confronted, but when we *talked* to Mrs Pike about their name. Names weren't really important to me, considering I'd only had one for my whole life and I usually gave other people nicknames anyway ('idiot' and 'plank' were common favourites) but their name meant the world to them.

They'd fought for it. Cried over it. Almost lost it.

A few long months later, their parents were semi-understanding and no longer threatening to kick them out, so we'd moved onto the issue of school. Nothing was legal, like, but it didn't have to be. That was what the 'student guidance counsellor' had told us.

I say 'us', by the way, only because they refused to go alone. They refused to do a lot of things alone, and it only took one look at their bitten fingernails and frayed hair to make me change my mind about trying to improve their independence. Not then. It wasn't the time for life lessons. After everything they'd gone through, and everything they were yet to go through, all they needed was a hand to hold. Often, that was quite literal.

They'd nearly squeezed my hand off in that tiny office. The walls were adorned with various motivational posters, the ones with nature and cute dogs and all sorts of random pictures alongside vague words like 'live your best life' and 'never give up'. The sort of thing that could apply to anyone and never be offensive. They were the walls that looked down on us when the counsellor said we could ask every teacher—every single one—if they'd use their preferred name.

Our conversation with Mrs Pike was a lot more recent than that one. We came in during break to talk to her, although she seemed a bit more interested in the Maths homework she was marking on her desk than us, if I was being honest. How someone could be at all interested in Maths homework was beyond me, but how someone could ever be a Maths teacher was also a mystery, so that might've just been a misunderstanding on my part.

Either way, she said she'd do it. She was going to use their preferred name when she took the register, and for the rest of the lesson. No big show, just a simple switch.

They'd collapsed into my arms as soon as we left the classroom, grinning from ear to ear.

"Danny?"

"Yeah."

"I'd appreciate a 'here', Danny."

"Yeah, I'm here. Miss."

"That'll do."

We were coming closer to their name. I was at the very end, but they were neatly in the middle of everyone. One curl of blond hair was wrapped around their finger, continuously twisting and untwisting.

It would be okay. I wished I could just go up

to them and hug them and tell them that it'd be okay, but even that probably wouldn't stop them worrying. All I could do was wait, just like them.

"Sarah?"

"Here, miss."

Closer and closer. For some reason, I was getting nervous myself. That was stupid. I knew she would use their proper name because she'd said so just minutes ago. I'd watched her lips as the agreement came out of them. Nobody forgot about a thing like that just ten minutes later, did they? I wouldn't, if I was a teacher.

Not that I would ever, *ever* be a teacher.

"Reese?"

That wasn't their name.

That was *not* their name.

She'd been told. My chair hit the ground, the front legs returning to the carpet. Moving my back away from the warmth of the radiator behind me, I waited for a second. Maybe she would correct herself. It was new, after all, you had to give people time.

A second passed. They didn't respond, because it wasn't their name. She didn't correct herself.

"Miss, that's not their name," piping up, because a silent classroom was always an opportunity to make a scene, I watched her eyes latch onto me. She didn't want this fight today, but I was ready to bring it to her.

"Please stop interrupting, Emily," she sighed,

THAT'S NOT THEIR NAME

shaking her head and looking back at her computer screen, "I don't want a repeat of last lesson. Reese?"

"You're calling out the wrong name," I pointed out, yet again, "of course they're not gonna respond."

"If this continues, I will have to give you a C1," with something like a smirk, she fixed her gaze on me. It didn't return to the computer. The fight had begun.

A C1 was nothing. A C1 was one stolen lunchtime and a text home, but I'd already briefed my grandparents on how little a C1 mattered. It would be worth it to make her spit out the name that was hiding behind her tongue. Their name was not Reese, and she knew it.

"Their name is not Reese, and you know it," uninventive at the best of moments, all I could do was repeat my thoughts, fighting the urge to jump up and stand on the table.

This wasn't the most glamorous of fights for equality, if it even was one, but I had principles. I stuck by my friends. I didn't let them get deadnamed by some stupid teacher who couldn't remember, or didn't care about, a conversation from the break before the lesson. I didn't really know which option was worse.

Probably not caring. Actually telling a teacher about their name change was one of their scariest moments. I'd watched them tremble in front of her. But, somehow, she thought it was okay to disregard their wishes and pretend we'd never even spoken about it? Sure, those weren't her exact words, but it was in the way she tried to dismiss me. It was in the lack of correction.

It was *everything*.

"I am going to try and do this register one more time, Emily," our eyes locked; we were truly stuck in the heat of a battle, and a sinking feeling inside of me told me it wasn't going to go well, "and I don't want you to interrupt it. Okay?"

"If you use the correct name for everyone then I think we'll be fine," not my best line, but definitely up there. It did nothing. There was no change in her face at all, but it felt like a little victory. Coming out and saying things was one of my only weapons on the battlefield of a classroom.

"Okay. Reese?"

"That's not their name," I repeated, figuring I had a few more minutes before I was sent out, "and you know that, because we had a conversation—"

"—I've had enough of this, Emily, you're on a C1—"

"—and their name is River, River, not Reese, and you were told—"

"—I won't hesitate to escalate this to a C2 if I need to—"

"—and all they want is to be called the right name, but you're just not—"

"Emily!" That was it, her breaking point. She'd had enough. The invisible line between us snapped. "You're on a C3; I'm calling senior staff to take you to a different classroom. You're disrupting the lesson and everyone else's learning."

"We're not learning anything, this is just the register," my point fell on deaf ears as she picked up a walkie-talkie on her desk and began fiddling with the buttons.

The person sat next to me started whispering about being sent out before the lesson even started, but I just shook my head and looked towards *them*. Sat at the front of the class, quivering. They probably thought they'd be hauled out with me or something, considering their view of high school punishment was pretty weird. They'd never been on a detention before—not even a C1—so they'd twisted the stories told to them by other students to create some monstrous impression of terrible detentions where you got tortured or something.

Something stupid. I'd tried to tell them that the only torture was being bored all the time, but they wouldn't listen. They'd never get a detention either, so they'd never learn.

The senior staff member arrived a few minutes later. I'd already packed my bag, smiling at the assistant headteacher who looked like he had a million better things to be doing than taking me out of my Maths lesson. River whispered something to me as I passed, but I couldn't hear them properly. My mind was blocking out all noise, turning words into nonsense and kicking them out of my ears. It always did, when I had to get up and walk in front of the whole class.

Believe it or not, this happened quite often.

Not always for such morally good reasons, since school and I just didn't mix, but that didn't change the fact that I was well-used to being carted from classroom to classroom when a teacher couldn't deal with my backtalk anymore. Or my empty worksheets. Or my fist in some student's face.

Yeah, I definitely wasn't a model pupil like River.

∞

Walking out of the detention hall (also known as the normal hall, just with a lot of chairs and desks and naughty students everywhere) at 4 PM was never a good feeling. My grandparents, while accustomed to the underwhelming effects of C1s, could still understand that being forced to stay behind for an hour after school wasn't a good thing.

The C3 texts were worded pretty heavily too, which meant a proper talking-to when I got home.

Drifting through the small crowd of delinquents, I made my way outside and across the yard, heading straight for the gates. I wasn't hanging around for any longer than I had to. I already had to come back tomorrow, and the day after that, and the day after that (unfortunately, school was a recurring event) so they weren't stealing any more of my free time.

Stepping over a patch of mud that never disappeared, no matter what the weather was like, I started down the short path to the gates. The visitor car park was on one side, containing a couple of heated arguments between the parents of the kids I'd shared my C3 detention with and the hot-headed kids themselves. Yeah, they *really* weren't happy. But a part of me thought that the silent cars filled with disappointed expressions and nothing else weren't much better.

My walk home definitely wouldn't be. Full of worry about getting home and facing my grandparents? Not a great way to spend half an hour, let me tell you.

But something was different. There was a figure by the school gates, and I didn't recognise it as one of the more zealous drug dealers who tried to get Year 7s to buy weed under the nose (and shiny hat) of the school's assigned police officer.

No, it was too small. The fact that it was dressed in a school uniform also led me away from the whole 'drug dealer' impression. Someone had a small friend waiting for them, I guessed, which was nice for them. It didn't usually happen that late into the year. People got bored with waiting around school for an extra hour every day, so the misbehaving friends had to walk themselves home.

Wait. Blond hair. Tiny.

I was so stupid.

"You didn't need to wait for me!" I called out, hurrying forwards a little. "Jeez, won't your parents be worried? You never stay out after school."

"Texted them," they replied simply, turning around and smiling softly as I arrived at the exit:

freedom, at last, "said I was hanging out for a few hours with friends."

"You? Hanging out?" Laughing, I shook my head and moved out of the way for a couple of people who seemed to be in a hurry to leave. Not that anyone wasn't, of course. "And they let you?"

"Not exactly," they shrugged, gesturing towards the road with their head, "but are we going?"

"Going... where?" Confused, I looked at the road and then back at them.

"Out. To the park, or wherever people hang out. For a few hours. Like I said?"

There was a little bit of silence between us while I digested what they'd just said. You have to understand, River was the complete opposite of anyone who hung out on the park after school. Their blazer was ironed every day. Their tie was the right length. Their hair, although messy, was always tied back for school. Shiny badges lined their lapels, detailing award after award after award. River did not hang out after school.

Was it because I stood up for them? Thinking about it, I didn't really do it that much. I'd never been allowed to meet their parents (by them) because I'd told them exactly what I'd say, and it wasn't very nice. But people generally left them alone, so I didn't have much defending to do. They moved through school like a studious ghost, leaving at 3 PM on the dot and returning at 8.30 AM to do it all again the next day.

"You having a rebellious day or something?" I asked, my wording awkward because I didn't really know how to say what I wanted to say. *Is it because of me? Is it because I spoke up for you? Was that all you needed, a little push? Why didn't you ever tell me?* "You're gonna be in trouble when you get home, if they haven't let you stay out."

"You'll be in trouble too, right? C3?" That was cocky, a little headstrong. There was something different in their eyes. It... it intrigued me. Who was this little alien who had taken over River's body? "We can comfort each other at the park. Or the smoking alley. There's one of those, right?"

"You're not smoking. *I* don't smoke," I corrected them quickly, before thinking about it for a second, "and there's five. That I know of."

"We can go to the park."

With that, they turned in the direction of the nearest park to school and began walking. Surprised, I had to speed-walk to keep up, but they didn't say anything until we got to the end of the road. Cars rolled past, some containing the annoyed parents I'd seen in the car park, as we waited to cross. They turned to me, almost shyly, their normal self visibly returning.

"Thanks, Em," they said, "I know names don't mean much to you, but..." trailing off, they looked up at me with large, lost eyes, and I nodded.

"Your name means a lot to you, and I understand that. Mrs Pike's an idiot, you know."

"Yeah."

The small smile that formed on their face was worth a thousand C3s.

Advice

One in three trans students are not able to be known by their preferred name at school. (Stonewall, 2017)

Getting deadnamed in school can be a big issue for us trans people, whether we've come out or not. Before coming out, you might feel conflicted between wanting people to use your proper name and putting yourself in danger or in an uncomfortable situation. That's completely normal. It's your choice if you come out in school or college or not, and no one can force you into doing anything. That being said, if you feel ready, coming out might be the next step to not getting deadnamed at school.

Most schools will allow you to have a preferred name on the register system before you've legally changed your name. You may need parental permission for this, so it may not be a viable option for everyone, but, if you're in a situation where you have (or don't need) your parent's approval, it can be a great way to relieve any social dysphoria around your deadname, at least in school. Registers become a delightful part of the day (for a few days or weeks, at least) when you can have your actual name read out by the teacher.

Unfortunately, this isn't the case for everyone. If you're not in the right position, you might not be able to get support from your school or college around your name change. Arguments and detentions are not the answer. Instead, try and build up a support system of friends who know and use your preferred name (and pronouns) at school. You might have to sit through a register which doesn't call you by the right name, but you'll always be able to go out to break or lunch and be called by your proper name. Try and console yourself with the knowledge that, one day, you will be known by your preferred name and be able to live as your true gender. Just keep going, and that day will come.

Resources

Websites

https://mermaidsuk.org.uk/ - **19 and under trans, non-binary and gender-diverse charity.**
http://genderedintelligence.co.uk/support/trans-youth/resources - **resources for trans youth.**
https://www.east-ayrshire.gov.uk/Resources/PDF/L/LGBT-Guide-for-Young-Transgender-People.pdf - NHS guide on many aspects of young trans life.

Hotlines

0808 801 0400 – Mermaids, transgender support for youth (19 and under), families and professionals.

Four Teenagers Sat On A Log

Content Warnings

Mild Arguments
Mention Of Drugs
Mention Of Unsupportive Family
Mention Of Tobacco Use

The River, it/its

"—and there were sixty-nine green bottles sat on a log—"

"It's fifty, you idiot!"

"I thought it was a hundred?"

"... is no one going to mention that it's on a wall, not a log?"

Amiable laughter rippled across the collection of four teenagers sat, as the song would suggest, on an old, thick log in a clearing by a trickle of a river. It grew much larger and deeper when rain fell, but it had been a warm summer and they were all grateful for it.

The river wasn't. Instead of actually rushing and flooding the earth, it was forced to trickle and drip like... like something sad. The river wasn't good with similes. Or metaphors, for that matter.

The teenagers were a unique bunch. One small, one tall, one round and one lanky as a rake. Judging people on their appearances was not a common habit of the river—apparently, the river had decided to be the narrator of the story, and so it began narrating its social opinions—but these four were so dissimilar that it had to remark on it.

Unknown to the river, they all had names. Names, backgrounds, families, loves, hates, relationships (or lack thereof). Senses of humour also varied, but all were appreciated. The river noticed that. No matter how bad the joke was, in its humble opinion, they all laughed. No matter how small the comment, they all noticed. They all talked and continued the conversation so that it never stopped but only ebbed and waved. It was something sort of beautiful to behold.

But the river was busy lamenting the lack of rain, so it only viewed them from a distance.

"What bottles are they, anyway?" One, the skinny one whose ribs pressed against his skin whenever he took his shirt off, asked.

"Milk bottles, innit?" Another, the round one who had an odd smile which uplifted and delighted all at once without anyone knowing why, said.

"Beer bottles," the small one corrected, "they're green, aren't they?"

"Don't ruin my childhood," the tall one smacked the small one around the head, but, despite the large noise, the teenager was unhurt, "it's just bottles. Plain old bottles. Sixty-nine green bottles sat on a log—"

"Stop singing! You'll ruin my ears, never mind your childhood!"

The river was quite in the same mind as the small kid—could it call them a kid?—since, despite not having ears, it didn't appreciate the singing. Not only that, but the song was being destroyed too. It had been 'sixty-nine green bottles' for as long as the tall teenager had been singing, which was quite a few minutes. A few minutes felt like an hour when it had to endure that singing.

Friendship was fine. It could handle watching, or listening to, a friendly conversation. Bands it didn't care about, people it didn't know, teachers it had never been taught by and places it had never been to. Perfectly okay.

A terrible song sung by a terrible voice? No. Just no.

It was sure that the tall teenager was a lovely person. It was sure that they had an okay life, okay friends and probably okay grades from the sounds of the conversation.

But an illustrious singing career?

Perhaps not.

No. *Definitely* not.

"Childhood's weird, innit?" The round one said. The small one cackled.

"You keep saying innit and you're gonna turn into an innit," they further cackled. No one was impressed.

"That was a serious comment, you idiot," the round one scowled, "I meant my childhood was a lie, alright?"

"Bit much for a Monday afternoon, May," the lanky one said, scratching the back of his neck with long fingers, the nails grown and jagged at the ends, "you feeling okay?"

"Bad GIDS session," the one who the river now knew as May replied simply, not elaborating any further.

It seemed that all the gathered teenagers understood, but the river had no idea what a 'GIDS' was or how you had a bad session with it. Was it a drug? Being a common teenage hangout spot meant that the river knew quite a lot about drugs.

It was strange that, for such a secretive-seeming topic, teenagers spent a lot of their time spouting off about this drug and that drug, the effects of them all and how to use them. Adults too, but they spoke a little quieter. Teenagers practically shouted.

It was a good thing that the nearest police station was an hour and a half away. The river had also learned that from the teens.

"My childhood was fine," the small one declared boldly, despite the earlier negative reaction to their comments, "just sweets and holidays."

"... and school, I'd hope, Kit," the tall one told the small one, named Kit. The river was learning quite a lot that day. A lot of useless knowledge, but gathering knowledge still felt important. Useful. Useless information felt useful? That was weird.

Almost as weird as teenagers.

"Well, mine was rubbish," May continued, unperturbed by Kit's comments, "coz we don't all have parents who raised us neutral, you know."

"Would that have made it easier, do you think?" The skinny one cut in, his question floating in the relative silence of the clearing.

Relative silence, of course, because the river was making its own noise. Water was never, and is never, completely silent. You think so? Put your ear to it. In it. Feel it. Drift a finger across its surface. The river's water was alive, always. Running. Listening. It lived. It existed. It forged a path through the earth and embraced every molecule of dirt it found. Every stone was picked up, petted and promised a better life further down, on a mossy bank which would look like perpetual summertime. The river was a dreamer.

It was also a liar. There was a bank—of course there was—but the stones would sink to the riverbed before they'd ever go near it. Only a few lucky ones ever felt the soft earth above the water, close enough to be springy but not drenched. The river knew that teenagers lied but didn't think that it had picked up that habit from them. Everything which could think, and which had a platform to voice its thoughts on, could lie.

"Maybe. Probably. I don't know," May sighed, shaking her head, "coz it never happened, did it? I got parents who hate my guts for everything I've done."

"Not what you've done; it's who you are," the tall one said, but May only started shaking her head more fiercely.

"I could just be trans and have never told them. That would be fine," she pointed out, "it was the telling that did it. That's why they hate me."

"They hate you?" Kit asked, semi-innocently, but there was something about their voice that wasn't quite right.

"'course they do. I was their model son, their perfect offspring," she stood up, swinging a fist at nothing, pacing, "Adam's a druggy and poor Lizzy can't do anything right. Bad grades, bad chores, bad attitude. Whatever can be bad is bad."

"You got a bad vocabulary," Kit laughed, not that anyone laughed with them, "just saying."

Although the river did not know a lot about the teenagers, since it was only a river and they were only teenagers, it didn't like Kit. The small one. A shock of red hair interrupted their blond mane, which could be called a mane since it was quite messy and in between long and short, that length which meant a haircut was due but not quite warranted. The price, or the time, always made teenagers hesitate until 'medium' became 'long'.

Then, parents usually intervened. Arguments and bargaining often ensued. The river had heard a lot of this.

Why the children disagreed with their parents was a mystery to the river. It had never had a child, nor a parent. Perhaps the clouds could count as its parents, but they never spoke so it could never speak to them. Arguments could not happen without communication.

"Look, you're still the same person, ain't you? No matter what they say, or if they hate you or not," the tall one said. The river felt like it needed a name for that one, since it agreed—or liked—all that they said. They were a teenage philosopher, but that didn't mean much. Most teenagers were philosophers, the river knew. It had to listen to them.

They weren't good philosophers, but they were definitely philosophers.

Life and all its mysteries were unravelled by the young, only to be forgotten once they got older.

Different things entered their heads. Bills, and mortgages, and jobs. Thoughts became facts. Lamented and criticised facts, but still facts. Teenagers dreamed, just like the river.

Adults smoked and complained. They complained about the material and the mundane. The everyday. They found something to moan about in their houses or their workplaces, their gardens or their pubs. Prices were raised, or shelves fell down. Bosses grumbled and foxes invaded. Adult life seemed miserable to the river, who only laughed and wondered when it would become an adult, if it would at all. It could have been a young or an elderly river. It wouldn't know the difference. The concept of age had next to no bearing on it since it only ran and never stopped.

"You're pretty cool for a straight guy, Matt," May returned to the log and pushed the small Kit out of the way, as the river decided that it had only one more name to learn before the afternoon would feel complete, "not that I'm meant to say that. Am I?"

"No," the lanky teenager promptly responded, after the question was left in the air for a few moments, "straight people deserve respect too. I think," he scratched the back of his neck, "I'm not straight so I wouldn't know."

"We all know that already," Kit said, a little too snarkily for the river's liking. The river had passed the peak of morality which it began the afternoon at and began to put its opinions into place. It felt sympathy for May. It respected Matt, even though it hated his singing. It didn't want to listen to Kit anymore.

The lanky teenager was a mystery.

"Kit, what's wriggled up your—"

"No need for that, Sticks."

Sticks?

Sticks?

Sticks was not a proper name. May, Matt, Kit and... Sticks? The river could barely believe it. That was ridiculous. Its knowledge was shrinking just at the thought.

Sticks. That was... that was underwhelming. Each name had brought with it something, some sort of emotion. Was it the name that it didn't like, or the character behind it? It knew the teenager called 'Sticks' wasn't straight, but that was about as far as its knowledge went. It couldn't work out which way its discontent went. The name, or the character? The name, or the faceless person?

Sticks was skinny. Sticks was male. Sticks wasn't straight. Sticks' ribs stuck out when you took his shirt off. There was nothing else. It felt emotion with everyone else, something, whether positive or negative. Why was Sticks neutral?

"Doesn't matter what we are. Who we are," Sticks said, almost on cue. Could the teenager hear the river? That would be an interesting development, "just that we're here."

"We're four teenagers sat on a log," Matt began, to a universal groaning which even the river joined in with, "what?"

"Don't start singing again!" Kit squealed, and the river thoroughly agreed.

Matt did start singing. Again. His song went 'four teenagers sat on a log' over and over and over again, until the sun began to sink wearily behind the horizon and the river rather wished, at once, that the teenagers would leave and stay forever.

While their speech was fine, the singing could disappear, never returning to existence ever again, and it would be very happy indeed.

Advice

82% of LGBT people are open about their identities to all or most of their friends. (GOV, 2017)

Having supportive friends is a great way to survive high school in general, but especially when you're trying to live your teenage life being LGBT+ as well. LGBT+ friends are great, since they're usually supportive and empathetic, as they likely know what you've been through or have gone through it themselves, but cishet (cisgender, heterosexual) friends shouldn't be looked down on. They're human, just like you, and they can sympathise, if not empathise, with your situation.

Besides, someone's sexuality or gender identity doesn't matter if they can tell a good joke that makes you smile on a bad day or remind you of that one time you did an amazing thing for them. Friends are friends. Luckily, most people report that they have supportive friends who accept them for who they are, but there'll always be a small minority who aren't able to have that luxury. Friends can be scarce, sometimes, and supportive friends? They're even rarer.

In the grand scheme of things, your situation might be fine. Out of a hundred friends (popular, aren't you?), you could have seventy or eighty supportive friends and only twenty that aren't supportive. Cutting off that twenty is no big deal. But if you've got three friends, and two don't support you? Things get trickier. Just know that every new life stage is an opportunity to find new friends, and there's a good chance they'll support you. Moving to high school, then college, then university, you'll meet fresh sets of people to like or dislike. Don't worry about a couple of bad friends now. Leave them behind and move on with your life; if you find a support system of good friends and keep adding to it and taking away from it as necessary, you'll always be surrounded by smiles and love.

Resources

Websites

https://www.consortium.lgbt/member-directory - a website full of LGBT+ groups in the UK. https://www.trevorspace.org - an online community for LGBT+ youth.

Dear Diary

Content Warnings

Mention Of Violent Hate Crime
Mention Of Physical Child Abuse
Mention Of Unsupportive Family
Mention Of Negative Coming Out
Mention Of Arguments
Mention Of Injury

Hunter, he/him

Hunter's Diary
Please stay out, I'd really appreciate it :)

17th September
Dear diary,

Super excited. Barely wanna write but I'm writing anyway, coz it helps, doesn't it? It does. I think. Anyway, really excited. Been talking with everyone—that's Luke and his mates, the nice ones I don't know yet but I'm really trying to be friends with them—and they think, from all that I've said, it's time. I'm gonna come out. It's gonna be amazing.

Well, not amazing. No cake or balloons or anything. But it'll feel amazing, I'm sure. Like a relief. Lots of weight lifted off my shoulders. That's what all of them say it's like—the ones that have come out, to their parents. Some of them haven't. One of them went all sad and quiet and had these big eyes but they wouldn't say a word. Like they wanted to say something, but they didn't. Luke hugged them afterwards.

But anyway! I am coming out to my parents tonight. We talked about it, us lot, Luke and his friends, and we think everything is right. I know they don't mind gay people, coz we see them on TV a lot and no one says anything. One of Luke's friends said his parents switched the TV off whenever there was a gay couple or anything, or switched it to another channel. Mine don't. Think that means we're all good.

Not much else to go off, but I couldn't give myself away before I came out and said it. That'd be the worst situation. Having them realise it on their own from me slipping up, trying to ask 'how do you feel about gay people?' without saying 'I am a gay person', but all that's fine now. No more planning.

At dinner. Once we all finish eating. Mum'll ask how school was. Dad listens—he doesn't ask but he listens and smiles. Coz I'm still getting good grades, like that 8 in science. Physics. Don't know how I got it but I guess midnight revision might work, no matter what Mr Yarder says. Was tired, though.

But dinner, I'm coming out after dinner. So excited. So, so excited.

Hunter.

Still 17th September
Dear diary,

Not sure how to write this. Everything went...

Uh...

Everything went bad. Very bad. As bad as bad can be. That sentence doesn't make sense but I'm writing it anyway. I don't know what to do. I guess write? Writing always helps, doesn't it? I guess. Nothing else can help now.

Dad got mad. Never seen him that mad. Got up. Stood up from the table, right after I said it and I stood up, so we were both stood up. I stood up first, like, to say it. I'm not making sense.

I stood up and said 'Mum, Dad, I am gay', just like I practised, and then Dad stood up and said 'no you're not'. I said I was. He said I wasn't. Mum stood up too and grabbed me across the table by the arm—she grabbed my arm, from the other side of the table, and took me out the room. Right outside. Outside the house.

She said I was wrong. Confused. She said I shouldn't have made Dad mad like that, for no reason, just some teenage phase. She was pacing and sighing and nearly crying at one point. Inside the house was silent. I think a neighbour looked over to see what we were doing, but Mum didn't care. She was just pacing. And sighing. And crying.

She did cry. Big tears. All the way down her cheeks, and they made me cry as well. I thought I'd be crying tears of joy, if anything, when I came out. But no. Bad tears. Cold and wet and whatever else tears are.

Stupid tears. I didn't know what to say and I told her that. She said I'd said enough. That felt horrible. Just shut me up, and I haven't said a word since. Can't. There's a big net in my throat catching all the words so they can't come out.

Went back inside. One of the lamps in the living-room was broken. The bit on top, the fabric-y bit, that was gone. Just the bulb left. It was turned off. I think Dad broke it.

I've never seen him that mad. I'm shaking and crying again in my bed because I don't know what to do. I said it. I came out and said it and he said I wasn't gay and I said I was and Mum said I shouldn't have said it at all. Luke and his friends said I'd be happy now. Free. Light.

I feel like I'm being pulled into a pit. I want to run away right now. Jump out the window. But I can't. I'm trapped. I'm thirteen. Thirteen. How many years until eighteen? Can you leave home at sixteen? At thirteen?

I don't know. I don't know. I don't know.

I'm scared.

Hunter.

18th September
Dear diary,

So. I came out on Friday. Today is Saturday. I thought nothing could get worse.

I sound so stupid.

Things can always get worse until you're dead. Unless torture is worse, I guess. I don't know. I barely know anything. Apparently, I don't know myself, because Dad keeps saying I'm not gay. He says it every time he passes me in the house, even if I haven't seen him for hours. Like at breakfast. I came down as he wanted to go up the stairs. Soon as I got to the bottom, he whispered it in my ear like some sort of secret.

Not really in my ear, I guess. That phrase is weird. He leaned down and sort of spat it, but he didn't spit. The words spat. No spit left his tongue. Or mouth. I don't think. It didn't hit me, anyway, so I didn't notice. He just kept bringing it up. Over and over.

I wish I never came out.

Luke said his went fine. Nothing fancy. I was almost modelling it after him. Modelling. That's a weird word to use for describing coming out.

Nothing could get worse. That was where I was.

171

Nothing nothing nothing could get worse, until it could. Coz it always can, can't it? I don't know why I'm talking to you. You don't care.

Why did I say that? You're paper. I'm sorry.

Why did I apologise to you?

Crazy. Everything's crazy. Dad hit me.

I said it. Like I said I'm gay. Mum said not to tell anyone. It's my fault. Kind of.

I don't think I wanna write about it today.

Everything's too complicated.

Hunter.

19th September
Dear diary,

Sunday. Days seem sort of important now. You know why? I can't go back to school until the bruise on my face magically disappears. Mum said. Dad went from never shutting up to finally shutting up and now he won't say anything. Not to me or Mum. He's like some sort of ghost. Stupid ghost. I hate him.

I shouldn't say that. You're meant to like your parents, aren't you? They give you food and clothes and a roof over your head and a bed to sleep in. Mine gave me a bruise. Mum screamed a bit but she didn't do anything. Nothing actual. She didn't stop him. With her hand.

Like she took me out of the room. When I came out. With her hand.

He didn't get her hand. She didn't take him outside. She disappeared. I ran upstairs. Dad went into the garden. I heard him muttering. My window looks out onto the garden, but I drew the curtains so I wouldn't see him. Or get light from his direction. But I'm upstairs anyway. I'm stupid. I don't know what I was thinking. I wasn't thinking.

I don't think he was either.

I'm always in bed now. Always. Luke texted. Asked. Probably coz I didn't say anything, coz I didn't know what to say. 'Your plan didn't work' sounds mean. 'It's all your fault' isn't the truth. So I left it. Now I don't know what to say. I'm leaving it. It's just a notification on a phone screen. It can't hurt me.

But...

Well.

I guess Dad can, now.

Hunter.

20th September
Dear diary,

Feel like I should do something. Heard Mum call school, told them I smacked my head on a glass door. Said it was a head injury so she wasn't having me in school. Think she thought she'd have a fight on her hands, like the time she tried to keep me off for feeling sick but they wouldn't let me off so I threw up in class instead. They didn't fight, though. Phone call didn't last long enough. She lied and put the phone down and came upstairs to tell me I'd be getting sent work. Email.

Still not looked at my phone. I don't know what to do. Dad gone all day. Work. Normal, I guess, but not normal for me coz I should be in school. I shouldn't notice him gone. But I do, coz I'm stuck here. In my room. Curtains drawn. The darkness seems safe, I guess. I don't know. I'm not thinking properly. Or at all.

I can't believe it. All this, coz I like guys. It's not a big deal. That's what Luke said, don't treat it like it's some massive something, just play it cool. Like a good grade you're proud of. Had plenty of those. Dad never hit me over it.

I never explained that. Guess I can, now. Here. In my

room. This isn't telling anyone if I'm just writing it down. I can write it and then burn it or whatever. It was my fault.

He said I wasn't gay. Again. Through the living-room. Was trying to sit down on the sofa, just watch some TV, and he said it.

So I said I was and he didn't know me and I hated him for that.

I think it was the 'hate' bit that did it. He stood up. I stood up. He stood up first, that time. Walked over before I could do much, or move. Couldn't move anyway. He was staring at me. Angry. He's never been that angry but all of a sudden he's furious in a couple of days for no reason. Well. I know the reason.

Then a bruise appeared and I cried and went upstairs to cry some more. Can't do much else. Mum said I can't tell anyone. I can't even bring myself to text Luke, or his friends. I have some of their numbers. But I can't.

Tore everyone apart over a sexuality. Thought they were alright with it. Apparently, gay people on TV weren't a good way to find out how my family feels about gay people in real life, AKA me—who would've known? Not me. Wish I did. Now Mum's sad and Dad's mad and I'm sat at home with a bruised face and some homework emails. Dark room. Dark life, right now.

God. I hate this.

Hunter.

Advice

94% of LGBT people who experienced a serious incident at home because of their identity did not report it. (GOV, 2017)

Coming out can be really scary for many reasons. One of the main ones is an extremely bad reaction from parents, either expected or unexpected. Even parents who seem fine with LGBT+ people in general might be unable to accept their own child being part of the LGBT+ community. This can be a terrifying experience. In the worst cases, this can lead to hate incidents and hate crimes within the home.

These incidents and crimes often go unreported. You may be literally unable to report them (kept in the home, threatened) or you may feel unable to report them due to fear of further repercussions, or what might happen next. If you can, it is best that you report hate crimes and incidents which happen within your home. This can be done through various means, such as the non-emergency police number (101) and other resources listed below. But it's not always possible.

So, what can you do? There are organisations, hotlines and charities which you can turn to for support. Or, if you have access to youth workers, trusted teachers or counsellors, you can ask them for advice. Be aware, though, that they have to safeguard you and information may be given to the police if they feel you are in danger. Don't let this dissuade you from getting help—if you are in danger at home, staying silent could mean you don't get help and the hate continues or escalates. Also, if you are in direct danger of being hurt or worse, always call 999. Being in genuine fear of injury is a real emergency.

Resources

Websites

https://www.childline.org.uk/ - Childline website.
https://www.letsendhatecrime.com - (Greater Manchester) if bullying escalates to hate crime, you can report it here (and also learn what exactly a hate crime is).
https://www.stophateuk.org/report-lgb-and-t-hate-crime/ - report LGBTQI+ hate crime and hate incidents.
https://www.theproudtrust.org/for-young-people/advice-and-support/ - advice and support for LGBT+ people.

Hotlines

999 - police emergency line.
101 - police non-emergency line.
0800 1111 – Childline hotline.

Me, My Girlfriend And God

Me, My Girlfriend And God first appeared in Star Gazette Magazine

Content Warnings

*Mention Of Unsupportive People
LGBT+ Inner Conflict Around Religion*

Freya, she/her

"Are you sure about this? You know you don't have to come if you don't—"

"Freya. We've talked about this. It's important to you, so I'm coming."

Smiling, I looked into the eyes of the one girl I loved more than anything in the world (such cliché, I know) and tried to figure out what was going on in her complex, unique mind. It was intricate. You could never quite tell what was flitting through her stunning, brunette head, but even getting close was an amazing experience.

She would do anything for me. I would do anything for her. I suppose that made us a pretty good couple, if you thought about it.

"It'll be like walking into a vipers' den," I mentioned, knowing I had nearly exhausted my list of metaphors but persevering nonetheless, "or a vipers' care home. They're all old. Most of them, anyway."

"Your mum isn't old," I knew that, and I knew that she was waiting in the living-room for us at that very moment, probably sat on her armchair reading a newspaper on her phone (which one? She'd never tell me, for some reason), while we hesitated and talked in the front garden, "and I've seen all the kids there. Not everyone who goes to church is old."

"The kids go to Sunday school, it's not the same thing," I shook my head, vague memories of being taught about the Bible and how to be a 'good person' in equal measure flickering uncertainly through my mind.

Childhood seemed like such a long time ago, even though I was still in it. Early childhood. Fifteen was still a child, wasn't it? Or was it?

The world confused me.

"We're in the eye of the storm," I pointed out, before correcting myself: "the calm before the storm."

"Can't even get your clichés right," she chuckled, reaching over to take my hand and squeeze it, "you're worried."

"Oh, you can tell?" I tried to match her chuckle, but it ended up being a half-hearted giggle, something that I would've come out with in primary school. Primary school... why did everything feel like such a long time ago? Why was I only realising that time passed in that exact moment? "We should go in."

So, we went in. Not much more to it. My heart was jiggling around in my chest as I jiggled the key in the door, like it was trying to copy me. Like a child.

Was I a child? Awkward questions which I really didn't need right then appeared, clouding my mind. Were they helping, by making me avoid the issue at hand? Or were they just being annoying?

Both. Neither.

We went inside.

The beautiful girl who I was incredibly lucky to call my girlfriend, sometimes called Teegan when I didn't have the energy to tell her exactly how much I loved and appreciated her just to address her, took her shoes off in the hall. I left my boots on. Mum didn't mind either way, but it was always something she commented on. From the first moment Teegan set foot in our house, took her shoes off and shook hands with my mum, Mum decided that she was 'the one'.

I had decided that a lot earlier, in a park on a dark night when she offered to walk me home. That was when I first noticed how her chestnut eyes glistened, so beautifully, under a yellow streetlight back when they were actually yellow—or orange, I guess—instead of electric white.

She walked me home. She made sure I was safe on a dark night, after an afternoon full of fun and an evening full of sharing secrets and memories. On that day, I knew her, and I knew she was 'the one'.

"Mum! We're ready," I called through the house, leaning against a wall as rushing sounds erupted in the living-room. 'Is it that time already' and 'I hope we're not late' floated through the house as keys clinked and the cat meowed indignantly at something. It probably got disturbed from its comfy position on my mum's lap, but church didn't wait for Whiskers.

It had waited for me. God had watched and waited as I struggled over whether or not to even go. Believing in him was never a question but believing that he still loved me after everything that I'd discovered about myself was. A lot of the people at church would have one simple answer for me: no. God didn't love lesbians, or gay people, or anyone who didn't fit the cishet norms of old Christianity.

But he loved everyone. Or he was meant to. I couldn't believe that I was living in sin when I also believed that God made everyone and looked at us as his own children. You only hated your child for being gay if you were a bad parent, and he couldn't possibly be a bad parent.

No. I believed in a God that loved me and all those old ladies just the same, no matter who we decided to spend our lives with or who we turned out to be.

He created me, after all, and he created me to be gay.

Mum appeared, frantically brushing her hair and checking it in the hall's mirror. Teegan smiled, greeted her with a compliment and looked about as calm and collected as I wished I could ever be. She was always like that. Teegan was just a calming presence, whether we were doing exams or getting yelled at in the park. Somehow, she managed to say the right things to everyone.

Finally, we all marched out of the house and into the car. Mum's urgency came in waves, which usually lapsed when she needed to do something like adjust her makeup in the mirror or look through her diary.

I think that was a parent thing. We'd always be in a rush until Dad needed to finish watching a horse race or football match on TV, when he was still here. I had a game I wanted to finish playing? Not important enough. Some men needed to kick a ball around a pitch with my dad watching? Completely fine, an extra ten minutes before we needed to leave appeared from nowhere. The logic boggled my mind.

But we all piled into the car in good time, meaning, at least, we wouldn't turn up late to church. That would be a good way to turn some heads, no matter who we were turning up with.

Of course, we were turning up with Teegan. That changed everything. But being late *and* bringing Teegan? Total disaster.

"Now, girls," Mum began, since it felt like the beginning of a long speech, as she started the car and began pulling out of the driveway, "I know that you know that this isn't exactly going to go amazing. It might not go badly, but neutral is what we're aiming for. I love you both, and I think you're perfect for each other and I'm sure everyone else, including God, thinks that too. But old Mrs Henderson—she's the one to look out for, I think—might not think the same. You're prepared for that, right?"

"Yes," Teegan chirped, cheery and calming as ever.

We'd gotten into the backseats of the car, so she reached over, again, and squeezed my hand, again. She called me out for my clichés, but she had a few old favourites up her sleeve as well. Not that I was complaining—the comforting touch of her fingers on mine, brushing the back of my hand in that way that she knew I liked, was incredible. Such a small thing, but still: incredible.

"Did you get your mock exam results, Teegan? I know you were waiting for them," and I was effectively excluded from the conversation. Part of me was relieved, since staring out of the window and watching the world pass by seemed like a great way to not think for a bit, or just think about some completely unrelated things, but I also enjoyed seeing my mum and Teegan interact.

It never got old. She swore that she loved us both the same, but I knew she really cared for Teegan. It might've been the best reaction to a new partner that any parent had ever had, ever.

I wasn't good with words when I was nervous.

To be honest, I wasn't great with words when I wasn't nervous either, but I was noticeably worse when something was on my mind. Teegan told me that. I'd not really noticed, being too busy worrying whenever this inability to speak properly thing happened, but she pointed it out one day. It made sense. She did that—I've already gone on about her so much, but she did so much. Everything about her was awe-inspiring. She was who I aspired to be, who I loved and who I wanted to spend the rest of my life with all at once.

As Mum and Teegan moved on to other school-related topics, such as the updated lunch menu (Mum and Teegan both had the ability to have extended conversations about pretty much any topic you threw at them), my thoughts wandered outside the car window. Houses passed. It was just houses and cars, houses and cars, then the primary school, then houses and cars. White car. Blue car. Black van. A lorry rushed past, gone in a moment. It probably shouldn't have been going that fast. One primary school kid in the road and then there'd be a real disaster.

But the primary school kids were at home, either in bed or eating breakfast. Or doing homework. I always did my weekly homework—weekly homework, what a blessing compared to high school!—on a Sunday. No one told me to, but I did it then anyway. Sunday mornings were for church and Sunday afternoons were for homework.

Sunday nights were for sleeping, just like every other night. Sleep was the best.

"Here we are," Mum announced, even though she didn't really need to.

The church was the biggest building in the area, and, considering it had its own car park, graveyard and gardens, it was pretty noticeable. Still, she said it, and it broke off my train of thought. All that pointless pondering, gone in a moment.

Back in reality, I got out of the car and drifted over to Teegan's side. Mum rooted in her bag for something or other, then checked that she'd locked the car three times. If anyone stole a car in a church car park... that would be low. A lightning strike would probably be on the way. Or at least some bad luck, I would hope.

The usual crowd was heading inside. Despite

what Teegan said, I was right. Mostly old people. Cardigans and jumpers and beige trousers, long skirts and wispy hair. I didn't dislike any of them, especially not just for being old, but I was wary of them. None of them had noticed us yet.

Would the car park change from being serene and filled with the general quiet buzz of chatter to a battleground if they did notice us?

Teegan didn't give me time to consider that doomsday option. My hand was squeezed. My mum found whatever she was looking for in her bag and locked the car for the fourth time, before coming towards us and nodding towards the door.

"We'd better head in," she said, smiling.

"Yes," Teegan nodded, knowing exactly what to say.

"At least it's not raining cats and dogs," I muttered, not knowing what to say at all.

All three of us walked into God's house, and I tried to not focus on anything but the thought of being welcomed by God.

Advice

32% of LGB people of faith and 25% of trans people of faith aren't open with anyone in their faith community about their identity. (Stonewall, 2016)

I'm not here to tell you if you should or shouldn't believe in whatever you believe in. That's completely up to you and relates to your personal spiritual experience, which I (obviously) know completely nothing about. I do know, however, that being LGBT+ can present difficulties around your faith identity and how you feel about not only what you believe in, but also the community centred around your belief.

Hopefully, your experience will be positive or neutral. It depends on your exact situation and religion, but it is possible that people will either not notice (introducing a partner as a 'friend' is something I have direct experience with, and it works if you can withstand a few hours without obvious relationship signs like hugs, holding hands and kissing) or not care. Realistically, attitudes are changing and people may just not have opinions on LGBT+ people participating in faith communities. You may experience a very positive reaction, too, from more progressive faith communities, and that's wonderful.

But knowing if there'll be a really bad reaction is also important. It could be possible that you live in an area with a highly anti-LGBT+ faith community, which you might have once been a part of. If this is the case and you want to attend that community's gatherings and events, keeping the LGBT+ side of your life private is probably the best idea. Trying to find different faith communities close to you is also an option, and there are some resources below to try and help you around that. If it's going to put you in danger, though, being private about being LGBT+ or not attending a faith community known to be anti-LGBT+ could be your best option. Overall, it's your relationship with what you believe in that matters, and that's a private matter—nothing to do with the 'old Mrs Henderson's' in your faith community.

Resources

Websites

https://www.stonewall.org.uk/resources-lgbt-people-faith - resources for LGBT+ people of faith.
https://sayit.org.uk/wp-content/uploads/2020/01/LGBT-Faith-and-BAMER-support-groups-1.pdf - LGBT
+ Faith and BAMER (Black, Asian, Minority Ethnic and Refugee) support groups.

First Impressions

Content Warnings

'Queer' Used As A Self-Identifier
Homophobic Language
Foul Language
Harassment

Eden, they/them

The day was perfect. There was nothing wrong with anything external, you see, just the human aspects of that nice, summery day. The park lived around us —me and August, my name being Eden and August's name being August—in birds, kids, squirrels, parents, teenagers... well, it was the teenagers that were the problem, but I don't want to focus on that right now.

No, there are two much more important aspects to that day. First? The beauty of it. I've always been an aesthete. August teases me about it, but I can't help being drawn to the prettiness of the world around me. On that day, that prettiness was everywhere. Almost everywhere, anyway.

I found it in the army of pigeons assembled by the pond, waiting to be fed by grandparents and grandchildren. Teenagers scared them away, but they always returned. The trees all still had their leaves, so they swayed and whispered and waved their sleek branches, dancing in some mystical way which no one but them could understand. Their secrets translated into the sounds of the wind. Bushes trembled, birds flitting into and out of them, sometimes pecking at the alluring red berries snuggled between spiky leaves.

After the beauty, there was the conversation. Here, I tease August—August is a sapiosexual, so they find themself drawn to the charming conversations we have on all sorts of topics. It's like a drug to them. A nice, non-dangerous drug, which I suppose doesn't exist in reality.

But on this day, this beautiful day, our conversation was brewing as we walked down the park's main path. It was wide and straight and led to a nice fountain at the end, with other, smaller paths splitting off from it at various points. We both knew it well and enjoyed being in its presence.

All we wanted to do was walk and talk. Nothing else.

Nothing more than that. It's not a human right or anything—not that I'm aware of, anyway, since August hasn't talked to me extensively about human rights before and my knowledge of them is a little limited—but it's not exactly asking for the world either. Why can two people not walk, hand-in-hand, without being harassed by teenagers?

I ask that and sound eighty years old, but it's true. For most teenagers, anyway. Not us, of course, although we were teenagers on that day, being seventeen and eighteen—I was the younger, and still am the younger, as that is how age works. We wouldn't be teenagers for too many more years, but it would be a substantial enough amount of time to convert ourselves into typical teenagers if we so desired.

We did not, in case you were wondering.

"Oi, what are you?" Out of the blue, a rather nasty sounding voice appeared, and we both looked up at once. In sync. That would have made me smile on any other day, had I not been suddenly looking at a puffy black jacket and a mountain bike, directly in front of us. It was not beautiful, I decided, so it did not enter my field of vision. Until it spoke. "You dykes or something?"

"No, actually," August responded, one eyebrow twitching—they hated ignorance, or stupidity, whichever it was. Both, I would imagine, but at least one was represented in that jacket and bike. "We both identify as queer."

"Fucking queers!" It yelled, the volume making me wince. "Get out of here!"

"Is this an anti-LGBT+ park?" I asked, although my tongue writhed in my mouth as I did so, nervous energy exciting it. Would we get attacked? Would it be like last time, near the McDonald's? Would we have to talk to patient but confused police officers about our genders and sexual orientations?

Hopefully not. That really would ruin the day.

"Dykes," was its final comment, as it zoomed away on the mountain bike.

Had it been with a herd of its own, it might have stayed, I theorised. Bringing this up to August as we continued on our way, abandoning the main path for a shadier and thinner side path, they nodded and agreed. Herd mentality and group confidence were dangerous, sometimes deadly, things, they said wisely. They often spoke wisely and still do, even when they're speaking complete nonsense.

That can be very amusing, especially after they've had a few drinks.

But we continued, nevertheless. We'd heard

MT

better, and worse. Hand-in-hand, we faced the world, and the world mostly smiled. We looked harmless enough that parents made their small children wave at us, since we were just odd enough to be identified as different, like a euro coin amongst the pennies in the fountain. It was the short hair, or the dye, or the piercings, or the clothes. Something.

Or it could have just been that they couldn't work out what we were, but instead of lashing out in their confusion, they tried to empathise. *Sympathise*. August wouldn't like me mixing those up. They couldn't empathise, because they—to the best of our knowledge—had not lived our lives, going through high school and then college as a non-binary queer couple.

It had been difficult, certainly, at times. It had also been a joy to have someone so close who understood the intricacies of my gender, and for them to have the same experience with me. Not quite all the intricacies, of course, as everyone is different, but most of them. More than the gist but less than the whole.

I need to mention that phrase to August; it sounds quite pleasing.

"There they are, the dykes—queers," at least it corrected itself but, that time, we did not respond. We did not look. We anticipated the same thing at the same time and turned into a small rose garden, with four benches stood around the flowers. Black iron sculptures twisted up through the grassy earth between the flowerbeds, their paint peeling and revealing the grey metal underneath. I turned my head for a moment, peering back the way we came.

The herd had arrived.

Although the rose garden may have been quite perturbed that we only chose it due to fear, or apprehension or whatever the exact name is for the feeling we were both experiencing, we did love it in our own time as well. On other days, we sat by the pink, white and red flowers to talk, and observe the occupants of the other three benches (when there were occupants, of course). It was quiet. It was shaded. It felt separate from the rest of the park, like a few other areas, but this one was the one we sat at. Not quite our home, but definitely a hangout spot.

This time, however, we did not want beauty. We did not look for interesting people to watch. Even our conversation had stilled.

The herd was following us.

"Do you think, Eden," August started bravely, reigniting our conversation and leading me through the rose garden, right through to the other side where another path led out of it, "they think about first impressions?"

"I don't see how that's relevant now," I said, completely unsure of where they were going with that conversation thread but more focused on the partially-bike-riding and partially-walking group behind us, clad in black jackets and tracksuit pants.

"Well, what will we be doing in ten years? Think of it as ten years or twenty years, whatever suits your answer. What will we be doing?" They asked, their breath a little disturbed from its usual pattern as we increased our pace, leaving the rose garden and hurrying down a winding path through gradually thickening trees. "We'll be in careers, right? Maybe advancing, maybe gaining some authority, some status. Potentially entering managerial roles, wouldn't you say?"

"Probably, although nothing is certain," I contributed, trying to feel the magic of our usual conversations, but the slow-paced chase continuing behind us really dampened the mood, meaning they had ruined the day in more ways than one, "and we may choose career paths without managerial options. Freelance, for example."

"That is true," they nodded, although I barely noticed it due to our movement. We got to the point in the trees where they stopped thickening and began thinning out again, signalling that another section of the park was approaching. "But if we are in managerial roles, they may be people who work under us, or—importantly—who we are involved with hiring."

"Would you hire any of them?" I asked, recognising as soon as the words left my lips that I wouldn't be able to recognise most of the group the next day, let alone ten years later. Even the initial spark, the bike and black jacket, was misty in my mind.

"Not if I recognised them, and there is my point," the trees thinned out further, allowing us to see the colourful children's play equipment in the distance, guarded by a dark blue fence, "they don't think ten years in the future. They don't wonder whether those people they yelled at and followed in the park will decide their futures ten years from now."

"They could decide our futures," I pointed out, "if they enter those managerial roles."

"That is equally possible," they said, only pausing for a moment to consider their following words, "but we did not chase them. They chased us. Thus, I don't know if the same negative connotations would exist for them with us, as exist with us for them."

Once again, the conversation paused. Without speaking further, we decided to walk through the children's park, hoping to shake off the crowd. That made the most sense. Children's play equipment was guarded fiercely by parents who seemed to love our brand of teenager (soft, round face, big smile, approachable, usually pastel coloured) and hate theirs, whatever it was. The fashion seemed to change every day.

Leather jackets, then waterproof jackets, then hoodies, then... well, whatever they wanted. They seemed to make it up as they went along.

August's hand reached the gate, pulling at the metal. It swung easily, well-used to being opened and shut by the hordes of young children who rushed through it every day.

The crowd's bikes squealed to a stop. Their boots stopped moving. They knew, as well as we knew, that the parents would not like them, but they would like us.

The gate clanged shut behind us and we walked into a haven. A noisy haven, full of sprinting little kids and parents on their phones, reading books and newspapers or rushing right after their offspring. One dog galloped around, despite the 'no dogs' sign just by the gate, but we didn't mind. We both liked dogs and the park could do anything at that moment.

It could become a den of unsupervised children, dog fouls and people hurling themselves into open water, for all we cared. We loved it as we loved the rose garden. We loved it for being safe.

"Just imagine," August sparked up the conversation again, leading us to an empty bench. I sat and breathed out a long, deep breath, emptying my lungs before filling them again, "the job interview. They come in. They sit down. You see their face as they shake your hand, and you remember—that day. The park. Their crowd—gang, herd, whatever you wish to call it. The memory is suddenly vibrant, crisp, fresh. *Negative.* And with that, the interview is soured. Even if you don't mean to be, you'll become more critical and look for reasons to discard them. That is what they have done, with their first impressions," they finished.

"Very insightful," I noted, "but I wouldn't remember their faces."

"You remember everything," they shook their head, extending an arm around my shoulders lazily, "don't doubt yourself so much. You know their faces."

"I don't," I interjected, "I don't know their faces,"

"You do, don't you? You know all of my friends' faces—even after one meeting, remember, you could pick them out? At the bus stop?"

"I know beauty," I asserted, almost pouting but stopping myself when I realised that gathering attention from lots of little children wasn't a good idea and reverted my face to a neutral position, "and I remember beauty. Any beauty. Natural, human, building. Architecture. Pets. Wild animals. Even squirrels," we had a joke about a squirrel once, an inside joke, one of the ones you only remembered by saying 'the squirrel thing' or 'the cake thing' or 'the school thing', but that happened so often that I usually forgot what the actual joke was, "but not things that aren't beautiful."

"You couldn't find beauty in their unity?" They questioned, raising their eyebrows. I snorted and shook my head, alarming a nearby child—a smile was needed to make them giggle and run away.

"Hate rallies aren't beautiful. Neither are lynch mobs," I sighed, shaking my head, "you can only take beauty so far."

"So, their first impression wasn't a beautiful one, on you?"

"Not in the slightest."

Advice

68% of LGB people have avoided holding hands in public, fearing a negative reaction from others. (GOV, 2017)

It's an age-old thing that nearly everyone must know about by now, but the fear around holding your partner's hand in public and being seen as a 'not-normal' couple by the people around you still lingers today. Not in every city, town and village and not in every public space, but it's still there. Some people don't hold hands when they pass large groups, or older members of the public, or while passing through a park. It shouldn't be the norm, but, for our safety, it often is.

If you find yourself getting harassed or followed because you and your partner are outwardly showing your relationship, or for any other reason, there are things you can do. Often, going on your phone and calling someone or pretending to call someone can put people off. If you can, find a safe space nearby—a friend's house, or even your own house, or inside a takeaway or shop. But, if you are in fear of getting attacked, call 999. This is especially the case if a large group has started actively following you and yelling at you or if you're far from home or in a new place you don't really know.

Hopefully, one day, we won't have to live in fear every time we walk down the street with the person we love next to us. As I said, in some places, that may already be your reality. But prejudice remains in our society, so you have to be aware of the possibility of negativity and what to do when you experience it. Try to stay alert. Be safe out there, in that wide, wide world—it can be a scary place sometimes, but all we can do is try to make it better for everyone.

Resources

Websites

https://www.letsendhatecrime.com - (Greater Manchester) if bullying escalates to hate crime, you can report it here (and also learn what exactly a hate crime is).
https://www.stophateuk.org/report-lgb-and-t-hate-crime/ - report LGBTQI+ hate crime and hate incidents.

Hotlines

999 - police emergency line.
101 - police non-emergency line.
0800 1111 – Childline hotline.

Looking Out For Olivia

Content Warnings

Mention Of Unsupportive Family
Mention Of Transphobia
Getting Kicked Out

Ben, he/him

benbenbenben
it's happened, guys

iamapillow
No way. No. No no no not today
not her birthday. He wouldn't.

Layla.Harvey
It's not just her dad. It's the sister too.
Nasty little devil spawn.

iamapillow
I thought it was demon spawn?

Layla.Harvey
It's both

benbenbenben
guys, kinda important thing going on?
she came to my house and now we're at the park,
tryna calm her down.

Layla.Harvey
OMG I'm so sorry I got distracted is she okay?

benbenbenben
she's got a bag and she's still got her job obviously
but her dad took her phone
he paid for it so

iamapillow
That's a jerk move.

Layla.Harvey
I wanna slap them both. Everyone in that stupid house.
They're all stuck up their own behinds they don't deserve her anyway, she's a gem
tell her that, Ben, please

iamapillow
Just to check, it is the trans thing right? Coz I never heard anything about her birthday being a deadline or anything like that.

benbenbenben
definitely the trans thing
she said he sat her down and told her that being eighteen meant he didn't want her under his roof anymore unless she 'stopped all the nonsense'
oh he took her makeup too, lots of clothes, she's not got much now

iamapillow
Oh god that makes it worse, it's always the small things that make you feel better and he takes those too??

Layla.Harvey
She can have some of mine. I've got enough for the entire town lol

she is coming to mine tonight right? my dad is next
to me waiting to get the car and 'save' her, you know
how he is
loves her more than me lol

benbenbenben
i think she needs a little time, but it's great that your
dad is still okay with the plan
about that, everyone still remember the plan?

Layla.Harvey
She stays at mine until she can rent somewhere?

benbenbenben
yeah pretty much, as long as she's presentable the
takeaway shouldn't care, she built up a bit of savings
like we planned, not much but yknow
it's more than i've ever had

iamapillow
Ngl i feel a bit redundant in this plan aha
Not complaining! Or anything, just saying I wish I
could help more.

Layla.Harvey
R you the same size as her? For clothes?

iamapillow
Maybe I'm not sure
I might be a bit bigger

benbenbenben
she says bigger is fine, you know how she likes
baggy clothes anyway

iamapillow
That's true. I'll check my wardrobe.

benbenbenben
your dad can probably set off in a few minutes, layla.
we're at the park by the billboard.

Layla.Harvey
Yeah, I thought so. That's in the plan too, isn't it?

benbenbenben
i love how no one remembers the really important
plan we made
it was only a few months ago

Layla.Harvey
Months are very long. And exams so shush
Dad is setting off now, I'm staying home to keep Lulu
company. She's prepared to give lots of love to
Olivia.

benbenbenben
she says she's looking forward to seeing you all,
especially lulu
this is crazy. i never thought it would actually
happen, yknow?

iamapillow
Yeah. It's like—parents aren't meant to do that,
they're meant to look after you
Not chuck you out at midnight on your birthday
How vile can you get? She was paying rent too,
wasn't she?

benbenbenben
ever since she got her job
think we can see your dad's car, layla, it's white innit?

Layla.Harvey
No, blue. Must be someone else.
I'm getting out the mattress now, it's just gonna be
next to my bed.
Does she need food?

iamapillow
It's midnight, she probably just wants to sleep

benbenbenben
yeah that seems to be the case, i'll wait with her until
layla's dad comes and then i'll head home

Layla.Harvey
He'll probably insist on driving you home too lol, you
know what he's like

benbenbenben
ya. he seems like the only consistent part of the plan
tbh

iamapillow
Found some clothes! I got jackets and t shirts and
some shoes and other stuff, idk what she needs
exactly but she can pick whatever she wants. Should
I bring them to yours tomorrow Layla?
Or today, technically, I guess

Layla.Harvey
Yeah, probably be dead until like lunch time though
I can only survive late nights at parties. I was
watching TV with my Dad, we were talking about
random stuff too, and it was nice but it almost sent
me to sleep

iamapillow
I'll set off at lunch time, then

benbenbenben
blue car is here
yeah it's your dad, only he waves like that

Layla.Harvey
What can I say? He's one of a kind or whatever the
phrase is

iamapillow
You literally said the exact phrase, don't doubt
yourself so much aha

Layla.Harvey
Shush, I'm tired

benbenbenben
alright guys, i think we're good. olivia is safe and i'm getting like a one minute lift home

Layla.Harvey
Everything's ready. Tell her I love her a lot, like, as a friend. What's the word for that?

benbenbenben
platonic?

Layla.Harvey
Yeah yeah that one

iamapillow
Me too.

benbenbenben
Thanks, guys. I love you all too - Olivia xxx

Advice

24% of homeless people aged between 16-25 identify as LGBT. (AKT, 2015)

Homelessness is a serious problem for LGBT+ youth. Being kicked out because you identify as LGBT+ can be terrifying, especially if you don't have an intricate support system like Olivia. If you're under sixteen, contact children's services through your local council. This doesn't mean you'll be sent anywhere you don't want to be—you could live with different family members, in emergency accommodation or with a foster family, among other options. You could also do this if you feel unsafe living at home.

For people who are sixteen to seventeen, you can still get help with your living situation. Contact children's services through your local council and you'll likely be provided with accommodation. They can assess your situation and see if you'll be able to go back home or live with a family member, but they will not force you to do anything or live anywhere where you feel unsafe. You'll be seen as a 'child in need' and offered help, so don't worry and don't feel afraid to reach out.

There are also charities and organisations you can seek help from, many being primarily LGBT+-orientated so they will understand your situation. These organisations may be more important to you if you're eighteen or over, since you have fewer options due to not being a 'child' anymore. But try not to worry. Seek out acceptive family members and friends you might be able to stay with, try to complete your education and aim to move into a job. Life is tough, but you'll be able to get through it. Stay strong. Accept help. Keep moving forwards.

Resources

Websites

https://www.gov.uk/your-rights-to-housing-if-youre-under-18 - rights to housing for under eighteens.
https://www.gov.uk/if-youre-homeless-at-risk-of-homelessness - help for if you are homeless or at risk of becoming homeless.
https://england.shelter.org.uk/housing_advice/homelessness/
help_if_youre_homeless_16_and_17_year_olds - help for homeless 16-17 year olds.
https://www.akt.org.uk/ - LGBT+ homelessness support.

Hotlines

0808 800 0661 – Centrepoint Helpline, free advice and support for 16- to 25-year-olds who are homeless or who are at risk of becoming homeless.
0300 330 5468 - Mindline Trans+, UK-wide helpline run by and for trans, non-binary, gender-diverse and gender-fluid people.

Talk To Me

Content Warnings

Mention Of Conversion Therapy
Mention Of Unsupportive Family
Mention Of Being Trapped In House
Mention Of Violence

TALK TO ME

Poppy, she/her

Call Connected

WREN
Hey babe, you alright? I just got off the bus, got work in a sec.

POPPY
It went bad. It went bad. It went so so so bad.

WREN
Babe? Are you safe? What do you mean?

POPPY
I tried it. Coming out. Like we said.

WREN
I thought you wanted me to be there with you? The whole 'meeting the parents' thing?

POPPY
Me too. I don't know. Mum saw my phone and I panicked. It didn't feel like the right time. But I had to. I'm sorry, Wren.

WREN
No no no, it's fine, it's fine, I'm more concerned about you? How are you? I'm guessing they didn't take it well?

POPPY

It's... it's really weird. I don't know. It creeped me out.

WREN

What? Babe, you're not making sense, how did your parents creep you out? Were they angry?

POPPY

She wasn't angry. You don't understand.

WREN

Okay, I'm sorry babe but I have to go into work, you can go to my flat and use the key under the plant pot to get in. Stay there and I'll call you on my break and on my way home.

POPPY

I'm sorry. I don't know what I was thinking.

WREN

It's okay. None of this is your fault. You're beautiful and I love you. Can you get out of the house?

POPPY

I think so. Dad is still at work. Mum's in her room. I'll get out.

WREN

Stay safe. I love you. Text me if you need me.

POPPY

I will. I love you.

Call Ended

∞

Call Connected

WREN

Hey babe, just got out on my break, how are things? Are you at mine?

POPPY

No. Mum stopped me. Said I had to wait until Dad came home.

WREN

You can't get out?

POPPY

No. No way. She's practically guarding the door. It's all so creepy.

WREN

Hey, what did you mean when you said your mum creeped you out?

POPPY

Did I say that? Oh. Oh yeah, she started speaking all weird. Calm. Like you'd talk to a child.

WREN
You are a child, babe. Sorry. Carry on.

POPPY
Eighteen is not a child. You're eighteen too.

WREN
Eighteen in a month is a child.

POPPY
Shush.

WREN
I'm sorry. What did she say, exactly?

POPPY
'I can fix you'.

WREN
What?

POPPY
She said 'I can fix you'.

WREN
You don't need fixing. God. It's 2021. What on earth?
I need to get you out of there. As soon as work is
over, I'm coming to your house.

POPPY

Please don't make a fuss, I love you babe I don't want—I mean—I don't know—

WREN

You don't want them to hate me? Bit late for that. She wants to fix you? She has to get through me first. Fixing, God, that's conversion! That's—that must be illegal. Don't go anywhere with them. Don't take anything they give you. I'll get you out.

POPPY

Please don't do anything stupid.

WREN

You know what's stupid? Trying to fix your child. Thinking you could ever fix your child, because—I don't know, I don't know, it's insane! What did you say to her?

POPPY

I just told her I'm pansexual, kinda explained what it meant and then said I have a girlfriend. Then she went weird and said the fixing thing. She didn't seem to care about you, though.

WREN

I want to kill her.

POPPY

Please don't kill her. She's my mum.

WREN

Parents shouldn't want to 'fix' their children.

POPPY

Please, Wren.

WREN

Okay, okay. I'm coming to get you after work, though. And if they don't let me, I'll come back every day until you're eighteen, then I'll call the police.

They can't keep you after that—I'm sure they can't.

POPPY

I'm sorry, Wren. I should have waited.

WREN

It's fine. I thought your parents were decent. Wait— when's your dad home?

POPPY

In an hour, I think. Why?

WREN

He might talk sense into your mum. Is he like her? Were there ever any signs?

POPPY

No signs. Nothing. I have no idea. I don't know. I'm scared. He might be worse. Who knows?

WREN

Keep calm. Just a few more hours until I'm out, then I'm coming. You'll be safe. Are you safe right now?

POPPY

I'm just in my room. Mum's still downstairs. The house is really silent and weird. She usually puts the radio on.

WREN

Okay. Okay okay okay. I've got to go back in again, but it's going to be okay. Text one of your friends— um, I think maybe Lewis will be good? He'll understand and he won't hesitate to call the police if he thinks you're in danger.

POPPY

Is that a good thing or a bad thing?

WREN

Good, in case your mum tries something crazy. Do you know what she meant by fixing you?

POPPY

She said she knew someone who could fix me, so she'd be able to fix me. 'It'll all be okay when she fixes me' she said. Things like that. A lot of that. She stroked my hair and told me it would be okay just like she used to when I grazed my knees or hit my head. But this time I was terrified. I was shaking.

Wren, I miss you so much—I need you here. I'm sorry. I don't know. I'm so confused.

WREN

It's all going to be okay. I love you, babe, more than the entire world. It's gonna take all the world to stop me from making sure you're safe, and the world's gonna fail if it tries.

POPPY

Okay, Wren. I love you. See you soon.

WREN

Hang in there, babe.

Call Ended

∞

Call Connected

WREN

I'm out of work. Waiting for the bus now. I'm gonna come straight to yours, don't worry.

POPPY

Dad came home.

WREN

How did that go? Did he talk some sense into her?

POPPY

He agrees with Mum. Says they can fix me, for my own good.

WREN

I can't wait to hug you and take you away from there forever.

POPPY

I haven't even packed anything. Forever? Do you think so?

WREN

For as long as it takes them to get those stupid ideas out of their heads. We were talking about living together anyway, right?

POPPY

Yeah. When my parents say I can.

WREN

Your parents want to fix you.

POPPY

Yeah.

WREN

Are we listening to their advice?

POPPY

I guess not. I hate all of this. Not you. I love you. But I hate being treated like a kid and being told I just need to be fixed. I don't need to be fixed. Do I? This isn't wrong, is it? Are we wrong?

WREN

Love is never wrong.

POPPY

Paedophilia is wrong.

WREN

Consensual love is never wrong. That's a weird comment for you to come out with, anyway.

POPPY

I don't know. I feel weird. I feel like I'm being watched by the world. The house is so quiet. The radio isn't on. I hate it. I hate everything. I want to leave.

WREN

You want to leave?

POPPY

Of course I do. That's all we've been talking about.

WREN
Yeah, but you really want to leave? And come to mine? And stay with me?

POPPY
Yeah yeah yeah, I can pay rent, you know, with my commissions money. It's not a lot but I'll find a part-time job too, and I'll—

WREN
That's not what I'm saying, babe, you'll always be welcome to stay with me. I'm asking if you really want to.

POPPY
Why?

WREN
Do you want to?

POPPY
Yes.

WREN
Pack a bag. Or two bags. Pack everything you think you'll need—laptop, phone, earphones, chargers, clothes, toothbrush, everything. The bus is here. I'll be outside your house in twenty minutes. I love you.

POPPY
I love you too. Please hurry.

WREN
I will.

Call Ended

Advice

5% of LGBT people have been offered conversion or reparative (repairing) therapy, and 2% have undergone conversion or reparative therapy. (GOV, 2017)

Conversion therapy, while rare, still exists today. People are still being offered, or sometimes forced into, therapy which tries to change them. We all, hopefully, know that this is wrong. No matter how the 'treatment' is done, whether it is some form of 'counselling' or something else entirely, it is wrong. To try and change someone to fit cishet norms is wrong. To make someone deny themself and not love who they want to love, or be who they want to be, is wrong. We are born LGBT+—we are born to become whatever we become, and no one should take that away from you.

Hopefully, we will soon live in a world where conversion therapy is illegal—or at least a country. Most counselling and health providers have said that conversion therapy is dangerous and they won't do it, including the NHS, but that doesn't change the fact that it still happens. What can you do if you're trapped in this situation, though?

Sometimes, it may be best to try and get away from the situation. For example, if you are older like Poppy and have a friend or partner's place to go to for a few days, that may be a good idea. Looking at living with different family members might also be an option. Ultimately, if you talk to whoever you are sent to for counselling or other conversion practices and clearly express that you do not want it to happen, this may work—but it may not. As always, if you're in danger you should call 999, and you can get advice and support from various LGBT+ organisations.

Resources

Websites

https://www.stonewall.org.uk/campaign-groups/conversion-therapy - information about conversion therapy.
https://www.theproudtrust.org/for-young-people/advice-and-support/ - advice and support for LGBT+ people.

Hotlines

999 - police emergency line.
101 - police non-emergency line.

No Peace

Content Warnings

Homophobic Language
Harassment
Arguments

Dylan, he/him

"You're such a fag."

    Inside the stuffy room we visited once every week, I sighed. Another hate crime presentation. Another evening of Paul jumping around in front of a PowerPoint, extremely excited about the prospect of teaching us all about hate crime awareness.

    We sat around him on chairs which were a little nicer than the ones we had at school, watching the projected slides as they zoomed and faded in and out of view. He always went all out with the animations. Despite being a simple rectangular room with long strip lights and thin, glass-covered slits for windows, it did feel a little homely. It was our community, I guess. Our safe space.

    Still, we yawned. We messed with crisp packets and looked out of the windows, seeing a city bathed in night. Winter did that. By 4 PM, darkness fell. It happened every day until spring came around again. You noticed things like that when you had to sit through the same presentation at least twice a year.

    "Now, we all know how to report hate crimes and hate incidents, don't we?"

    Hate incidents. Those were the odd ones, the ones I couldn't quite remember whenever Paul called on me. He was so much better than a teacher, though—he had to be. He was a youth worker. They encouraged you and helped you to learn, even though there was no final exam or grade at the end of everything. Just a better person.

"There's the website, guys—what's that website, Jayden?"

"Let's end hate crime dot com," Jayden groaned, slouching further into his plastic chair, "just like it was last year and the year before."

"Less of that, this is important," Paul said, shaking his head, but a smile played on his lips. "I'm glad you remembered. Let's end hate crime dot com, everyone, and if you don't want to use the website? Eve?"

"101," Eve spoke simply. He was satisfied.

"Exactly. Let's end hate crime dot com, 101 and if it's an emergency, if you're in danger, if someone's coming towards you and they're going to attack you, if you're unsafe at home—call 999. Emergencies need 999."

This didn't need 999. Some idiot from the year above didn't warrant such a response. She didn't even know, probably, that she'd just committed a hate incident.

No crime.

Just hate.

A verbal slur, or whatever Paul would call it. If he was watching me, he would be pointing towards my phone, or the nearest staff room, or something. He wasn't, though.

The real world wasn't a small room with a bright presentation on a projector. It was corridors and lockers and cheap, gum-filled carpet; ceiling panels that had been popped out so many times they had permanent gaps between them; bathrooms full of graffiti but devoid of any toilet roll.

That's where I was. Not the bathroom and definitely not in the ceiling, but on a thin corridor jammed with students. They wore maroon blazers that nobody really liked and swung around their sometimes-designer bags like brutal weapons. A thousand faces passed by me, young and curious and, for some of them, mean.

She was mean.

Not only because of the slur, but also because she didn't leave. She'd washed up with a wave of kids, positioned herself by my locker and called me out for being a 'fag', despite the fact that I was an asexual biromantic person, not a 'fag'. No one was a 'fag'. Fags were cigarettes.

I had yet to find a person who truly resembled a cigarette.

But then, she wouldn't leave. She stood there, a head taller than me, and stared. No more words. Nothing. Just staring. Staring and staring and, for some odd reason, not leaving. Out of all the people in the world, fate had to send this stupid Year 10 or 11 or whatever she was towards me and she had to lash out for absolutely no reason. I'd never done anything to her. I'd never even looked at her.

But apparently, I looked 'different', or 'cigarette-like', so I had to be commented on.

"Why don't you just do the world a favour and die?" That was a bit of an escalation, and she knew it. She leaned on a different leg and crossed her arms, her head tilted a little to the side. A question, expressed in body language: *what are you going to do about it?*

Not much, I tried to silently respond. I wasn't in the mood.

"You're unnatural, all of you. Your little gang. I've seen you," she said that like it was some sort of threat, but I saw hundreds of Year 10s and 11s—I still didn't know which one she was—on a daily basis, hanging out with their friends. I mean, I even saw them smoking in the alleyways on the way to school, but I never said anything. It seemed like existing was more of a crime than underage tobacco use.

Oh, that sounded posh. I was really getting annoyed.

"You all hang out and squeal and hug each other and kiss and whatever, but you'll all go to hell for it. If there is hell," now she was confusing me, switching from ultra-religious to agnostic in a heartbeat, and I started to wonder if this really was about me, "because if there is, it was built for you."

"Shame I don't believe in it," was all I could say. Lame, I know, but she was tall and mean-looking, and I didn't want a fight.

To try and get this across to her, I shut my locker firmly and turned to look at the rushing crowd of students flying past, trying to get somewhere. They all wanted to be somewhere. No one actually wanted to stand in the corridor, not if they were alone—you looked out-of-place. You looked like a target. You moved in the corridor, or you got called a cigarette by an ultra-Christian-agnostic person.

Yeah, high school really made sense.

"Remember, guys, you don't have to report a hate crime or incident if you don't feel comfortable doing it. Other people can report it for you," Paul continued, clicking to the next slide of the PowerPoint with his magic little remote.

"Question," someone—I looked around and saw it was Millie, the soft-spoken, skirt-wearing person, going by female pronouns that week but not always, who sat in the corner a lot, "what if no one was around when it happened?"

"If you tell someone that it happened, they can report it," grinning, which probably would have seemed a bit odd to anyone who wasn't used to Paul's style of presenting, he took a few steps forwards, "second-hand, third-hand, fourth-hand, fifth-hand, as many hands as someone can have! As long as they know about it, they can report it. Teachers, parents, friends—anyone you want."

The next slide was the website, again. 'Let's end hate crime dot com', as we all referred to it, although the actual URL didn't use 'dot' as a whole word. That didn't matter. Sometimes, I wondered if any of it mattered. I'd never experienced anything remotely like a hate crime. Hate incidents? Maybe. But didn't everyone get called bad things at some point or other?

It was different, though, if you got called a bad thing because of the six protected characteristics. We had six, but not everyone did. It was us, in Greater Manchester, and a couple of other places. It sounded complicated, but all it meant was that Sophie Lancaster's death led to alterophobia being recognised as a form of hate crime or incident—in plain English, discriminating against someone for being from a subculture, like goth or punk or... yeah, I didn't really know a lot of subcultures. It was good that we had it, though.

Loads of other places just had the basics. Gender or gender reassignment, for trans people, sexual orientation, ethnicity, faith and disability. There was the whole thing about 'you don't have to actually be it as long as someone discriminated against you because they thought you were it', too. That sort of confused me. If someone called a straight person a cigarette, that would be a hate incident too, because the name-caller perceived the straight person as being gay, or whatever else. When you got into specifics, it got confusing.

Luckily, Paul was prepared to teach us all about it at least twice a year, so all I had to do was wait a couple months for the hate crime presentation to come out again. Problem solved.

"You don't care about going to hell, fag?" She really wasn't going to let it go. She took a step forward as I took a step back.

The people around us were oblivious, chatting and hitting each other with bits of paper (if you folded paper a certain way, it became a weapon —don't ask me how, I have no idea) and getting told off by similarly oblivious teachers for not having their shirts tucked in, or their ties in the right place. Turns out that 'around your head like a ninja' wasn't in the dress code for how to wear your tie, as one Year 7 found out.

"Not really, considering it doesn't exist," I countered, turning around and rolling my eyes. I didn't need this. On top of everything else that was going on, I didn't need this. She didn't need to know that. She shouldn't have said anything in the first place. But I... I just wanted her to understand and go away.

"Wait," her hand was on the back of my shirt, *her hand was on the back of my shirt*, was that a hate crime? Not quite, I didn't think. Not yet. Her fingers wrapped around my grey collar, which was meant to be white. It used to be. A long, long time ago: the start of Year 7. "You really don't care?"

"I don't give one," snapping, I struggled out of her grip and turned back on her, trying to make my face look as frustrated as possible—that wasn't hard, considering I was pretty frustrated already, "because life is hard enough right now, while I'm alive. I know I'm alive. I can touch my arm and see that it's real, that all of this is real. You, unfortunately, are real. Hell is whatever—hell is some dark pit no one knows about. I'm not denying myself the freedom to love who I want just because some pit might not like me kissing a guy, alright?"

"Sounds like one long excuse for being a homo," she shrugged, but she wanted to get away. I saw it. Something in her body language, something that I wasn't clever enough to label but knew instinctively. "I don't care. Go to hell if you want, fag."

There was no victory. There was no heroic final speech. There was no last word. There was only her fading into the background and me rushing to the toilets to lock myself in a cubicle and breathe. I cried, but I didn't know why.

Poetry written in marker pen accompanied my weird emotions, along with a delightful collection of all the swear words the males of the school knew. Some additions were actually quite interesting. It took me a few minutes, but, eventually, I could read them through non-blurry eyes, tracing the lines with one finger.

Against the harshness of the newly painted white cubicle wall (the graffiti artists of the student body didn't take long to catch up and paint the walls once again, this time to their liking with felt tips and biros which scratched more than they drew), my finger seemed like something I could hold onto. It contrasted with the white, making it clearly visible. I could see it. I could touch it, with another finger. It was real.

She was real too, but she was gone.

My phone was real. The memory of her hung on my fingertips as I opened the web browser. Fag, fag, fag, fag, how many times had she called me a cigarette? How long had I stood there?

Her fingers on my collar.

I struggled away. This was serious. Serious? It was. Was it? It had to be. I was shaking and wiping away tears in a dirty toilet cubicle, while she swept off to wherever she spent all her free time. The backfield. The benches. Somewhere without the memory of me clinging to her.

She haunted me. Her breath was hot on my neck; her fingers bunched up the back of my shirt; her voice was cruel and cold. Mean. I had to do something.

She couldn't think that what had just happened was okay. She couldn't.

Let's end hate crime dot com.

Pause. Hesitation. Enter.

Advice

A hate incident is any non-crime incident which is perceived by the victim or any other person, to be motivated by a hostility or prejudice based on protected characteristics. (ATP, 2021)

High school might have numbed you to hate incidents. It's not your fault, but sometimes—especially when it's happening to other people—you might hear slurs and hateful comments and barely raise an eyebrow because teenagers can be really crude people. Hopefully, your teachers notice and stop this behaviour and language, but they might not. They may look the other way, or simply not notice. What can you do, then, if you are verbally targeted due to one of the five/six (depending on your area) protected characteristics?

First, a refresher. The five main protected characteristics are disability, gender or gender reassignment, sexual orientation, faith and ethnicity. These can be actual (you're disabled and someone uses an ableist slur) or perceived (you're cisgender and someone uses a transphobic slur). Both can be reported. It's also true that you can report hate incidents first-hand, second-hand or any other number of hands, as Paul says, as long as you know something about what happened.

There are various methods for reporting hate incidents. Don't use 999 unless you're in danger (i.e. you fear being physically attacked, robbed, etc.) but, instead, use the non-emergency 101. Another option is the various websites you can use to report hate incidents, or even going into a police station if you're comfortable doing so. Even if you just pass on information to someone else who reports the hate incident, you're helping in the fight against hate.

Resources

Websites

https://www.letsendhatecrime.com - (Greater Manchester) if bullying escalates to hate crime, you can report it here (and also learn what exactly a hate crime is).
https://www.stophateuk.org/report-lgb-and-t-hate-crime/ - report LGBTQI+ hate crime and hate incidents.
https://www.consortium.lgbt/member-directory - a website full of LGBT+ groups in the UK.
https://www.trevorspace.org - an online community for LGBT+ youth.

Hotlines

999 - police emergency line.
101 - police non-emergency line.

Out Of The Closet, Into The Party

Content Warnings

Mention Of Deadnaming
Mention Of Alcohol
Mention Of Drugs
Mention Of Underage Drinking
Mention Of Violent Hate Crime
Mention Of Unsupportive People
Mention Of Violence
Mention Of Violent Weapons

Zoe, she/her

"Okay, do I need to go over this again?"

"Not really, love, but you can if you want to."

Pacing back and forth across my purple carpet (specifically chosen to be purple by me because purple was almost pink and almost blue, and I overthought everything) I looked to my partner with what can only be described as an 'exasperated' expression. I hoped it was one of those, anyway, because that was what I was going for.

Parties never used to be this confusing. Parties, of all things, should have been about relaxing. Chilling out, underage drinking and probably some drugs somewhere—not that I ever touched them, obviously. Neither did Ash.

But he didn't like parties as much as me. He'd sit in a corner and watch people get drunk and fall over, then start chatting with their parents (if they were home). Parties sent him right into his little politeness shell. It was interesting, if a bit unusual, to watch.

"So, my name is...?" Waiting for him to finish the sentence, I stopped pacing. He turned a little red and shrugged, fidgeting as he sat cross-legged on my double bed. Purple sheets. Galaxy. Purple and red and blue, just to make everything even. "Ash?"

"Well, that's not my name tonight, is it?" He was right. But that wasn't important—him remembering his own 'name' that he would have to use was fine, but he also had to remember mine. I was more worried about that. "I don't wanna say it, Zoe."

"Not Zoe," I reminded him, but I couldn't bring myself to actually say the name which stuck to my tongue. It felt wrong. "Just—maybe we shouldn't use names?"

"That's not how people work, love," he pointed out, flopping backwards onto my bed. His fluffy hair splayed out over my galaxy pillows. Purple doodles and ink stains looked down on him from the white ceiling—white, pure, completely neutral. "Hello, I'm no one and this is my partner, no one, we'll just get some drinks and sit down while no one talks to us because they're confused and we sound like weirdos."

"Shut up," I sighed, sending him a weak smile to make sure he knew I was joking.

Well. Half-joking, anyway. This whole situation was driving me crazy. My bedroom light flickered, the warm yellow glow gone for half a second, but that was enough to settle it in my mind.

It was a bad omen.

That fraction of a second spent in blue darkness, where the intricacies of the galaxies around us couldn't be seen anymore, was enough. I didn't want to go.

But, at the same time, I did. I really did. It was Sophie's birthday and she always had a party. I always went. Without fail, I'd show up every year and get introduced to all of her friends, who would forget about me as soon as alcohol turned them tipsy. I always brought a little present—this year, chocolates (last year was also chocolates, and the year before) —and, sometimes, a partner on my arm. This year wouldn't be different in that regard.

Except for the fact that it was getting dangerously close to driving me completely insane. Neither of us were out to anyone at school about being trans, so Sophie still thought I was... well, the name I went by when everyone thought I was a boy, and she—if she knew that Ash existed—thought Ash was the name he used to go by when the world saw him as a girl.

That complicated things.

Obviously.

I was out to my parents and Ash had barely needed to come out to Phil, who basically told him that he knew from 'day one', but school?

No. No one knew. We wanted it that way, but it still sucked and made everything confusing.

Parents and foster carers were one thing. They were predisposed to love us and take care of us and not mind when we messed up or revealed that we weren't what they thought we were when we first got taken out of our mothers'... well, you know what I mean. Horrible imagery, I know. I apologise. But it was true. They took a bit of time, accepted the change and kept on loving us, thankfully. It could've turned out worse than that, but it didn't.

School, though? None of those teens had any reason to love us or accept us. They had quite the opposite, actually, since we knew none of them but they were predisposed to hating anyone 'different'. A Year 11 boy came in with one earring and left with a black eye and a ripped ear lobe. The assembly on hate crime was booed over and ended before it even got properly started, with half the hall being sent out and straight down the corridor to the headteacher's office. They threw the free bibles we were given all over the place and slashed up the pages.

It didn't matter what it was; if it was different, it was bad. Bad things were feared. Fear led to destruction.

I didn't feel like getting stabbed by a drunk teenager, so we were playing it safe.

Safe meant confusing. Safe meant hurting. Safe meant deadnames which we didn't even want to think about being uttered out of our own mouths. That was different from a teacher saying it, or a friend who just didn't know. It felt like we were betraying ourselves. Ash wasn't as bad about his, but he absolutely hated using mine. I knew that and I felt so bad for making him do it, but we had to.

I wanted an alive boyfriend, not a dead one.

"Not being out at school is exhausting," Ash rolled over and nearly fell off the bed, swinging his arms around to balance himself. He ended up in the middle of the bed again and sat there looking at me. "Isn't it?"

"Yeah. Hiding all the time sucks."

It felt like we were in some fantasy book where magic was outlawed, so we had to hide our magic, only the magic was being trans and outlawed actually meant 'not socially acceptable'. Not in our school, at least. Not for the first time, I wished we lived anywhere else.

Well. Maybe not anywhere else. But somewhere better.

"But we can't take chances," I continued, turning away from him and rooting in my wardrobe (purple), "and you know what everyone's like."

"Not everyone," he said, flopping onto the pillows again, "not Sophie."

"Not Sophie, but her boyfriend? He'd stab you," the casualness of my words shocked me, but that was what high school did. It numbed you.

I'd heard Michael say those words so often ('I'll stab you', 'I swear I'll stab you', 'I'll stab him', 'I'll stab her', 'I've got a knife', 'I'll prove it', etc.) that the thought of them didn't do anything to me. He never said them to me—just to most of the other students we shared a school with. It didn't change anything, though. I wasn't scared of the words.

The knife, however? Definitely. I'd seen it a couple of times. A little silver thing, black handle, blade flipped up when he was showing it off. Probably illegal. Just long enough that he couldn't hide it completely in his hand. Kept in his inside blazer pocket. Revealed to brag or threaten. Or impress Sophie. Any occasion, really, was an excuse for Michael to get his knife out.

I was hoping that this party wouldn't be another one.

"Alright, next problem," side-stepping the deadnaming issue, I flung open one wardrobe door for dramatic effect, wincing as the new hinges squeaked angrily, "what are we wearing?"

"What do we usually wear?" He asked, not moving from his position face-down on the bed.

"Hoodies," despite the fact that I really didn't need to tell him that he was currently wearing a hoodie, I reiterated that point anyway, "but we can't wear hoodies to a party. Can we?"

"What did you wear last year?" He asked, and I scrunched up my forehead trying to remember. Last year—Year 8—was a long time ago. "A hoodie?"

"No," I sighed, for the hundredth time that evening, and pulled out an armful of assorted clothes. Dumping them on my motionless but still talking boyfriend (no cause for concern, just laziness), I started sorting through them before I realised I didn't know what I was looking for. "Last year I wore a polo and jeans."

"Fancy," he sat up again, sending a few shirts flying, and started thumbing through the rainbow of fabrics, "so we can't put you in a dress, because 'men don't wear dresses' or whatever," his air quotes made me laugh, but even the reference to me being seen as a 'man' chilled my stomach, "but we can't put you in a polo and jeans because you'll look ridiculous."

"I will not! Is that your only objection to polo and jeans?" My outburst sent him flopping back onto the pillows, waving his arms in defeat, as I hunted through the pile and found a non-offensive pairing of a polo and jeans. "This is fine. Girls wear pants."

"And polos," he added.

"And polos, thank you," frowning at him, I threw the clothes to the side and started piling everything back in the wardrobe.

I hated parties. At that moment, anyway. I missed turning up in clothes I spent a minute choosing and just having fun. On the park. In someone's front room. Back garden. Field. Even the little parties we had in the hall at primary school were fun, with a tuck shop which apparently adhered to inflation over my seven years at the school. I missed being outraged at the prices of those sugary treats, packed away in plastic or grabbed with scoops from tubs and put into tiny paper bags, or cups. The music that we thought was good. The hall that we thought was massive. The lights that we thought were awesome.

Life really did peak in primary school. From there, it all went downhill.

Once my clothes were back in the wardrobe, I perched on the side of my bed and felt two reassuring arms snake around my chest, pulling me onto a carefully manufactured pile of pillows. Girlfriend trap, Ash called it, and he always seemed to pull it off without me noticing. I guess... I guess it was because he only did it when I was stressed, and I always missed things when I was stressed.

One time, I focused so much on putting down the right name on my exam paper that I didn't write in the date. I stressed about revision and brought a blue pen to lessons instead of a black one. I spent hours choosing clothes for extended family gatherings (only my close family knew I was trans) and ended up leaving my phone at home.

Something always slipped. I couldn't hyperfocus on one thing without ruining something else.

Falling back onto the pillows, I tried to go through some sort of mental checklist as Ash peppered my face with soft kisses. His lips were always so gentle and... no, no, he was distracting me. I stared up at the yellow light and tried to think.

Present? The chocolates were on the desk.

Clothes? I'd picked out a polo and jeans.

Phone? On charge, sat on the bedside table.

Bag? I was taking a backpack, practical and unisex.

Boyfriend? He was heavily distracting me from the checklist with affection.

Boyfriend's clothes?

Oh. That was it. At least one of the things that I had forgotten. Ash had shown up at my house in a hoodie and tracksuit pants, and I thought nothing of it—that was what he always wore. They were his dysphoria-safe clothes, baggy and neutral, dark-coloured and non-irritating on his skin. But he couldn't go to a party in a...

Wait.

"You're not going to the party in a hoodie," I giggled a little at the absurdity of it all, and the fact that I'd found out what I'd forgotten before we had to leave, which was a little victory for me, "you *cannot* show up in a hoodie. Sophie will kill me."

"But it's a designer hoodie!" He protested, launching backwards, falling off the bed and then rolling around on the floor for good measure.

"It's not. Take it off," I crawled towards the end of the bed and looked down at him as he rolled about, smiling, "do you also want a polo and jeans?"

"Do I have any other choice?"

"Nope."

"Jeez, being trans sucks," he complained, sitting up and leaning back against the bedroom wall.

"No," I shook my head, sitting back as well and letting my hands escape into the soft material of my galaxy bedding, "hiding being trans sucks."

"True that, love. Gimme a polo, then."

Advice

76% of non-binary people, 59% of trans women and 56% of trans men have hidden their gender identity, fearing a negative reaction from others. (GOV, 2017)

In some situations, you may feel the need to hide your identity from others. This could be friends, parents or even strangers. Not being out might be your safest option in many situations, such as high school (not always the most accepting of places) or a non-LGBT+ friendly family. That's fine. Don't feel any pressure that you 'should' or 'need' to be out. Your priority is your safety.

For trans people, this can be particularly uncomfortable. It could include using your deadname, since many schools will only change your 'preferred name' on the register with your parents' permission and deed polls require parental permission if you're under sixteen. It's tough being young and trans. But you can get through it. Seek support from friends who accept you, or online communities of fellow LGBT+ young people. You don't have to be completely alone.

Hiding a partner can also be hard, taking a mental and practical toll on both of you—how are you meant to pretend that you don't love each other? Can you hug? Can you hold hands? At a base level, insisting that you're only friends may be enough to make people leave you alone, but being aware of avoiding physical intimacy could help. Hold on and wait until you can truly be yourself; it won't be long.

Resources

Websites

https://www.mind.org.uk/information-support/tips-for-everyday-living/lgbtiqplus-mental-health/lgbtiqplus-mental-health-support/ - LGBTIQ+ mental health support.
https://www.gov.uk/change-name-deed-poll - information on deed polls.
https://www.princes-trust.org.uk/help-for-young-people/who-else/housing-health-wellbeing/wellbeing/sexuality - LGBT+ resources.
https://www.consortium.lgbt/member-directory - a website full of LGBT groups in the UK.
https://www.trevorspace.org - an online community for LGBT youth.

Hotlines

01273 72 12 11 – Allsorts, free helpline for young people under 26 who are lesbian, gay, bisexual, trans or unsure (LGBTQU) of their sexual orientation and/or gender identity.
0207 700 1323 – Pace Youth, free and confidential counselling for LGBTQ youth under 19.
0300 330 0630 – National Lesbian And Gay Switchboard, support and information for LGBQ people across the UK.

Orange Day

Content Warnings

Mental Health Services (Counselling)
Low Mood
Mention Of Overbearing Family

ORANGE DAY

Layla, she/her

Her room was always warm. The radiator was silent, which was weird since I'd only ever known radiators that were noisy and covered in black and orange and brown spots. Oh, her—she was my counsellor. Emma. I forgot her last name all the time; it was too long to remember.

The white door shut behind me. She was already moving to sit in one armchair, which had been positioned to face the one I would sit in. Some people liked to sit on the floor, she'd told me in our first session, leaning against the radiator or looking up at the window. I chose the chair. I always did—it wasn't much of a choice. More of an acknowledgement of the other options, followed by a dismissal.

She'd only asked on the first day. After that, she knew I'd just sit on the armchair.

"How are you doing today, Layla?" She asked, settling down and crossing her legs. A few papers were scattered over the coffee table, one looking suspiciously like a questionnaire. I'd filled in enough questionnaires in the past few months to put me off them for a lifetime. "Green, orange, red?"

"Orange, today," I said, wandering towards the armchair and perching on the seat. I'd relax, once we got started. I usually did.

It was just the thought of my mum waiting outside in the waiting room and the lingering, suffocating embrace of a long day of school that had me... 'off'. I said that a lot. I felt off, something was off, the day felt off. Everything was off, sometimes.

Emma must have been sick of me saying that.

"So, what made today orange?" She had a certain voice that she always used, which wasn't quite the voice that spoke to my mum in the waiting room. Just part of her job, I guessed, but it was nice. A comforting touch, soft and smooth and gentle and all the other nice adjectives. "School? Home? Something else?"

"I don't know, really," I admitted, crossing my legs and looking out of the window, "I just woke up and felt off, you know," there it was again, 'off', but she didn't say anything about it, "but nothing happened, not really. That's why it's orange."

"Yes, you've mentioned that," she nodded reassuringly, reaching over to the coffee table and pulling one of the papers off it: notes, "green is waking up fine and staying fine, orange is waking up not fine and staying not fine, and red is waking up not fine and becoming worse throughout the day. I do like your system. It's very... neat," she remarked.

"Do other people have similar things?" I asked, wanting to divert the conversation away from me for a little bit, just to get some breathing room.

"I can't say anything specific," she started, and I expected that—I knew about privacy and confidentiality, "but giving you the control to make your own mood system, or any other tracking system, is a beneficial technique. We use it a lot here," she smiled, a sweet smile which encouraged me to let down my guard during my first few sessions.

I didn't want to go to counselling. Counselling was for... well, I didn't know who I thought it was for. Not me. Not the kid everyone ignored until they couldn't see me smiling every day. They wanted a smile. They wanted a wave. They wanted a joyful greeting, or a hug, or something.

I couldn't deliver.

My mum said it was gradual, but, to me, it was just how I'd felt forever. I used to care, a little. I used to pretend that I was happy. That got exhausting. Don't get me wrong, I didn't have some sort of massive thought process going on about the whole thing. I was barely through primary school when I gave up—barely conscious.

That's the thing, about early childhood. It seemed real at the time, but all that reality drained away once I got through year after year. I wasn't thinking. Not in Reception, not in Year 1, not in Year 2. Year 6 was on the cusp of conscious thought. But it wasn't quite there—none of those years were me.

I'd tried to explain this to Emma, once, but I think I confused her. I couldn't blame her. She was only a person, and my explaining process wasn't great.

"Is there anything specific you'd like to talk about today?" Her question was normal. I must have heard it once every session, at least.

"I think..." mulling it over for a little bit, I looked outside and watched a squirrel dart across a tree, my mind temporarily blank. It recovered, and I came up with something. "I'd like to talk about my mum."

"Great," she said, "we've covered your mum a few times before—would you like to continue one of those conversations, or is there something new you want to explore?"

That one took a little time. She understood. I shuffled back in the chair and moved my eyes back inside the room. Radiator. Coffee table. Two armchairs. Both occupied. The ghost of a woman began to form on the other side of the room. Was 'ghost' the right word? Maybe vision. That woman wasn't dead.

She was sitting in the waiting room.

I never really understood how my mum felt about my counselling sessions. She'd been all for them at the start, until I refused to tell her about anything that happened in them. Emma assured her that she'd be told if there was a safeguarding concern, but there'd never been one. In reality, the sessions would just be boring to anyone else.

She wanted to know about them, though. Intensely. She'd referred me to the service, then waited to hear about it every day when I came out. She waited. Then waited some more. After a bit more waiting, she got demanding. That didn't work. People demanded things off me all the time, but I just shut down and ignored them. Pressure did nothing to open me up—all it did was send me into a shell.

My mum had discovered that a long time ago,

but she kept pushing. It was like she didn't learn, or she didn't want to learn. I didn't care. Not caring was something that I was incredibly good at. But not caring about my mum pressuring me led to not caring about my mum, and that was a whole other issue.

"I want to continue one," I said, deciding to take my thought thread and pull it out into her room, "the one about counselling. Kinda meta, I guess."

"I remember," she smiled, putting the paper down and replacing it with another one, "I brought an information sheet, just in case this came up. It seemed to be bothering you quite a lot last week."

"Thank you," once the sheet was offered to me, I took it, looking down at a blue and yellow mess of 'child-friendly design' on 'pushy parents', basically, "I didn't think you'd have one for every single possible situation."

"Pretty much everything you can think of has an information sheet," she said, as I read through it and resisted the urge to roll my eyes—none of it was anything that I hadn't already thought of. Useless. I put it down on the coffee table and shook my head, as she sighed. "No good?"

"Nope," I replied, "just stating the obvious."

"How would you improve the sheet, then?" She asked, opening an obvious avenue into actual counselling, but I didn't mind. That was what I was there for, even if I didn't like it at first. That was what she got paid for. Counselling. Not casual conversation.

Casual conversation was nice, though. It just had to happen at the right frequency—not too little, making her unfriendly, but not too much, making her useless. She had to be a counsellor, and I had to work with her. If I didn't—as she told me at the start—that was fine, but we wouldn't get anything done and the sessions would be a waste of time for us both.

"I'd improve it with some actual ways to help," I didn't mean to snap, or sound ungrateful or rude, but my words came out as they came out, "I mean, all it says is basically 'talk to your parent and explain how you feel'—that's about as useful as saying just talk to a bully and explain how you feel and become friends, but that doesn't stop you getting punched in the nose and getting your bag stolen at lunch, does it?"

"I suppose you're right," as always, she was agreeable and encouraging, as she had to be, "so what would you add to the sheet?"

"I don't know. I'm not a professional," I said, shrugging.

I was beginning to shut down. Pressure. Questions. I hated questions which had any sort of weight to them. They terrified me. What do you think, how do you think, why do you think—they were all terrible. School was hell for them. Getting called on in class was the easiest way for me to retract into my safety shell. Safety shell... that sounded like something Emma would come up with.

"That's fair enough," she was moving on, trying to get past the block, but I was fully prepared to keep my mind and thoughts hidden for the rest of the session. She'd pushed the wrong button, in the wrong way, at the wrong time. It wasn't her fault. Or maybe it was, for not being a mind-reader.

Mind-readers would make the best counsellors.

"How does your mum feel about your identity?" That was a bit of a shocker. It made me sit up and stare at her for a few seconds, wondering if that question had actually left her lips. It had. This was cold reality, where exams, disgruntled parents and counselling lived.

"I don't know how *I* feel about my identity," I reminded her, as the 'questioning' label practically floated above my head. Sometimes, that made me feel a little inferior—everyone else had their identities figured out. Granted, most of them were cishet, which was a pretty easy conclusion to come to in most cases, but me? Fifteen years and I still couldn't look in my head and heart to see what sort of identity lay there. All I saw was a black mist which encompassed the shell I loved and hated, all at once.

My life was just one long metaphor, existing to be picked apart by parents and counsellors.

"Yes, but how does that make your mum feel? Do you talk about it?" Lots of questions, direct questions, but they were bold and interesting and— new. Different. Was this some sort of tactic, to get me talking again?

It felt like an electric shock. I couldn't blame

her for doing her job, but it did feel weird.

"We don't, usually," I said, "just because there's not much to talk about. I don't know who I like, if it's anyone or no one, and I'm not even sure what I am most days. Maybe I'm asexual or demisexual, maybe I'm trans or gender fluid, maybe I'm straight and cis—who knows? My feelings are all over the place. One day I feel like I might finally have the answer, but it slips away. I can't tell her that," I tried to bring myself back to the question, knowing I was getting off-topic, "because I can barely think about it without getting a headache. So she just knows I'm a bit confused, and that's it."

"She knows you're thinking about everything, though," Emma said, with her usual smile, about to pop out a profound line that would stick with me until the next session, "and that's progress. That's opening up, even if it doesn't feel like it, and that's what we're working on. Gradually unravelling those layers until we find where you're comfortable—your sweet spot."

"My sweet spot," I repeated, rolling the words about on my tongue (non-verbally, so I didn't sound like an idiot), wondering if that was it. It wasn't her best, but it wasn't her worst. That was okay. She was just a person, I had to remember, just a normal person. "We're not there yet?"

"Not quite," she said, "but we'll get there. It might take time, but we *will* get there."

Advice

28% of LGBT people found it 'not easy at all' to access mental health services, and a fifth had negative experiences when they accessed them. (GOV, 2017)

Accessing mental health services can be really scary. It's a huge step which can feel like a massive wall between you and recovery. But being LGBT+ can make that huge step feel like a formidable mountain. Young LGBT+ people face so many barriers and obstacles while growing up: your parents might not understand or accept you; your friends may reject and ridicule you; your school may shut you down or ignore you. If mental health issues start to crop up, help may feel like just another problem on top of everything else.

Confidentiality plays a big part in this. If at all possible, try to either get assigned to a counsellor (specifically a counsellor, not a student advisor or a teacher burdened with extra responsibilities) who is trained to deal with mental health and other issues. They are trained to help you and should know the difference between, for example, reporting a safeguarding issue and unnecessarily outing you—your LGBT+ identity is not a safeguarding issue, by the way.

Another issue you may face is, to put it bluntly, variations on 'you're depressed because you're gay' or 'you're anxious because you're trans'. This can seem horrible the first time you experience it, but you may not experience it at all and all you need to do is power through it. It can be helpful to explore how your identity affects your mental health but communicate and ensure that the right issues are being addressed. Once you make that leap and get access to mental health services, keep talking and try and get the most out of it.

Resources

Websites

https://www.mind.org.uk/information-support/tips-for-everyday-living/lgbtiqplus-mental-health/lgbtiqplus-mental-health-support/ - LGBTIQ+ mental health support.
https://www.theproudtrust.org/for-young-people/advice-and-support/ - advice and support for LGBT+ people.
https://www.nhs.uk/using-the-nhs/nhs-services/mental-health-services/children-and-young-peoples-mental-health-services-cypmhs/ - NHS mental health support for children and young people.

Hotlines

0207 700 1323 – Pace Youth, free and confidential counselling for LGBTQ youth under 19.
116 123 – Samaritans, confidential support for people experiencing feelings of distress or despair.

Reaction

Content Warnings

Mention Of Suicide
Aftermath Of Suicide
Grief
Mention Of Bullying
Mention Of Deadnaming
Mention Of Misgendering
Mention Of Unsupportive People
Mention Of Violent Hate Crime
Mention Of Self-Injury
Mention Of Drugs
Mention Of Tobacco Use
Mention Of Mental Health Services (Therapy)

REACTION

Sam, he/him

"If there is any support we can offer you—anything at all—if there's anything you want us to do, or you think we should be doing, you can talk to us. Everyone will listen to you. We're here for you. We'll get through this sad, *sad* event together, yeah?"

He didn't care. I looked straight into his big, I'm-So-Innocent-Ofsted-Please-Don't-Put-Us-In-Special-Measures eyes and knew he didn't care. There was no emotion behind them. That room, that tiny office which they shoved us all into, was full of emotion. It stank of grief. But he didn't care. He didn't feel anything towards Taylor.

Maybe, if he called Taylor by their proper name and used their proper pronouns, I could almost believe the whole sympathy, We're-All-In-This-Together approach. Maybe.

But, as things stood, it was the biggest load of empty words and promises I'd ever heard. Just the same as when he stood up in front of the whole school and told them he wouldn't tolerate homophobic, biphobic or transphobic bullying. We tried to go to him, after that. We tried to tell him.

We got turned away. Me and Taylor. We tried, but he didn't care.

All they did was react. A kid got beaten up for being trans and they did an assembly. Taylor... Taylor did what they did, and we all had a cute little meeting where they pretended they were going to do something.

It wasn't just him. Mr Guinn was the headteacher, and the headteacher had lackeys. Our head of year, Mr Dane, was shaking his head, his arms crossed over his chest. That was his sympathy. It was all he could muster. The same look that he gave to misbehaving Year 7s in the corridors, or talkative kids in his maths class.

Do you know who cared? Miss Wright. There were tears in her eyes. Those hard eyes which scrutinised our science papers term after term were filled with moist emotion. Trembling emotion. One tear slipped down the side of her nose as she tried to take form, speaking the words which had been fed to her through a formal email from Mr Guinn. She knew Taylor. She was the first to call them Taylor, out of all the teachers, and she tried her best with their pronouns. They knew that.

It wasn't easy. But the ones who cared tried, and lots of them just didn't care. They didn't want to know. If it wasn't on the register—and, with Taylor's parents, it never would be—then they disregarded it. Even the ones who called 'Jonathon' by his nickname, 'Johnny', couldn't bring themselves to use Taylor's name. Hypocritical? Maybe. I didn't know. I didn't have time to know or even think.

I'd spent the last five years trying to support Taylor in a world jam-packed with hate for them.

For someone who came out in primary school, they had a lot of trouble getting people to believe them. They knew too early, or too late. They were confused or persuaded. Most people had unique-seeming responses that fell into a few lazy categories. They didn't understand. They didn't want to understand. They actively rejected them. They tried to be nice but fell into a different category anyway. Barely anyone accepted them.

I did. From the first moment I met them, I knew I wanted to be their friend. It wasn't perfect—life never is. My confusion over them introducing themself as 'Taylor' when the name the teacher called out was completely different took a few weeks to fade away. For some reason, I kept getting in trouble for calling them Taylor in Year 8. Only Year 8. I think there must have been some sort of discipline boom in Year 8 that disappeared by Year 9, never to be seen again.

But we were friends. Mates. Best mates. I knew their parents, and their parrot that never shut up, and their favourite food (it was the rice that came in packets; it took two minutes in the microwave and then got covered in ketchup). Not many people knew that. Not many people got close to them, out of fear of getting bullied or confused. Or taught something, I guess. People wanted to believe that boys were boys and girls were girls and no one could be anything in between. Being friends with Taylor directly challenged that.

High school kids hated being challenged.

Whether it was tough maths questions or new identities, they detested it. That's a sweeping statement, I know, but it was true for most of the people I met. Some of them could handle 'gay'. A handful dealt with 'bisexual' like champs. But the numbers got fewer and fewer as you went more obscure until all that was left was a community of coarse-language loving students who lashed out at the first sign of anything new or odd. Sheep? No, that's cruel.

But they were cruel to Taylor, so perhaps they deserved it. No one bothered me, not directly—I got the usual gay questions when I started hanging out with them, but even in Year 7 I didn't care about that. I knew who I was. Straight and cis, and there was nothing wrong with that, just like there was nothing wrong with Taylor being non-binary. They didn't lean either way, masculine or feminine, but they told me some non-binary people did and that was okay too. They just wanted to be true neutral. No, they *were* true neutral. They suited it, too.

None of that mattered to Mr Guinn. None of that mattered to Mr Dane. None of that mattered to the majority of people at Longwoods Academy that day, when they were herded into a suicide awareness and prevention assembly.

I got to skip it. He understood how to act like he cared, so Mr Guinn sent me to the library for the day. No lessons. Just worksheets and books. To give him a little credit, he'd made an effort to get to know the Year 11s, even though we'd only been in our last year for a month. He knew I liked reading. It was the bare minimum, but he knew it.

Maria was allowed to stay in a small computer room, meant for the IT staff, and Marc got put with her just because Mr Guinn couldn't send him to the smoking alley outside school. I know he would've gone there in a shot. I would say that I thought he snuck off anyway, but he wouldn't leave Maria, and Maria wouldn't smoke. He loved her more than cigarettes, which is depressingly romantic.

Little Vivienne was taken out of the room by the school counsellor, Helen. Sobbing. Hands over her red face. Chewed fingers. I didn't want her to be there. She shouldn't have been told like that. As soon as the announcement left Mr Guinn's mouth, she looked like she'd been blasted in the chest with a shotgun. Her face fell. Her eyes darted around—to me, to the teachers, to Marc, to Maria. There was outrage, as she read our expressions and realised we already knew. Then understanding—we hadn't told her because she was vulnerable. Fragile. We handled her with kid gloves for every situation because we knew she needed it.

Our little group had formed at the end of Year 10. It was a funny story which didn't feel right to discuss, concerning the state of us at that moment, but it did involve the canteen and a spilt lunch. Vivienne was mortified, Maria was angry and Marc was guilty. Taylor and I had cold chicken pasta all over our laps.

Since then, we'd spent a hazy summer living life like teenagers approaching their final exams. No revision, obviously, because reality didn't work like teachers wanted it to. We weren't about to shut ourselves in our rooms and pore over textbooks while the sun blazed outside.

Marc had a part-time job and Vivienne had her weekly therapy sessions (technically, she had two separate therapies which alternated weeks, but we referred to them all as therapy) but we still managed to hang out. We sat in trees and ran across fields and petted nice dogs in the park. Sometimes we ate at my house, but everyone loved eating at Vivienne's—her aunty made the best pie, and that summer was full of it.

Then, school arrived. With a crash, our summer was gone, replaced by a cold academy which didn't care about us. Exams, exams, exams. Hate, hate, hate. The combination was deadly. It took Taylor from us.

But we would always have that summer. Those memories were sweet, tinged with sunlight and fresh grass and apple pie. They were beautiful.

∞

I left the office last. The world was full of echoes as I walked down grey corridor after grey corridor, different emotions swirling around my mind. Sadness, of course, and grief, but then came anger. Nothing I was looking at had taken Taylor away from me, away from the world, but I felt like it had. Everything was grey—depressing, of course they hated it. Reminders about exams were posted on every wall—pressure, of course they hated it. Stupid kids with their stupid haircuts and stupid jackets they weren't meant to wear inside—hate, of course they hated it.

Why would anyone want to stay here?

The library was up a set of stairs, the sense of antiquity bearing down on your shoulders as you arrived at the top. I loved it—or I used to love it. On that day, it just felt like one burden on top of all the others. Usually, Taylor would be at my side, making some joke about books and nerds and being quiet in libraries. I almost convinced myself that they were there.

But I turned my head to the side, saw nothing but a new suicide prevention poster on the wall, and told myself off for hoping.

Just for a little variety, I focused my mind on reading the poster, diverting my path from the double doors which opened into the library to the noticeboard on the wall beside them. Various failed clubs had pinned handmade posters to that board, accompanied by curt reminders to tuck your shirt in and take your coat off. But the new poster had been placed in the centre of them all, partially hiding Chess Club and Trainers Aren't In The Dress Code.

'Reach out for help! You're not alone! Speak to the student advisory officer for a referral to Longwoods' official counsellor!'

The words were plastered all over the A4 piece of paper. Blue, pink, red, green. Friendly colours. Soft and pale and non-alarming. This was their 'trying'. This was their 'effort'. This was how much they cared about Taylor.

A stupid poster that would get torn down before the week was up.

Turning away from it, I found a different thought kicking around in my head. Taylor never got angry. It was sort of their thing; they were chilled out constantly. The sort of person who seemed eternally high, even though they never touched drugs. People spat at them, kicked them, stole their bag and yelled at them, but they never responded with anything close to that level of violence. It was almost the opposite. If they were a Christian, they would have been the perfect example of turn the other cheek. The perfect person.

They *were* perfect. Perfect in that human, flawed way, as no one can truly be perfect, but you knew as soon as you talked to them that they'd be a good friend.

All this past tense was going to get tears running down my face again. I'd been through that. I'd sat there on the phone with them, then called the police when I was genuinely afraid that they'd do it. I was terrified. I was crying with my mouth wide open, biting my knuckle so hard it scabbed. All I'd done, all I'd said, all I'd tried—it wasn't enough.

But they wouldn't want me to be angry. They wouldn't want me to be bitter. School was terrible, but we both already knew that. Happiness. They'd want peace and happiness like they always did, so I walked right up to the library doors and slipped into the huge room with the high, beamed ceilings that were covered in cobwebs. Hopefully, they didn't stop Taylor looking down on me and seeing that I was functioning. I was still living. I could live, for them.

Maybe those posters would save someone's life. I had no way of knowing. As ever, I was too tired to try and figure things out. But, if it did help someone, then great. Longwoods finally did something.

Taylor's legacy was built out of suicide prevention posters and assemblies, but at least it was something. I had my memories, but I also had concrete, tangible things to hold onto. That was... that was something.

Tears began to run down my face, again.

Taylor...

Advice

One in eight LGBT people have attempted to take their own life in the past year. (Stonewall, 2018)

Suicide is never an easy topic to talk about, or read about, or see on TV. This can be especially true for people who have lost a loved one, or who are battling with suicidal thoughts themselves. Losing someone is devastating. There's a hole in your heart where they used to be, and all sorts of guilty or grief-stricken thoughts might mess your mind up, sending you into saddening spirals of despair and 'if only' cycles. Battling through being in such a bleak and hopeless state of mind can also be difficult. How can you ever get past suicide, or overcome suicidal thoughts?

Everyone deals with suicide and its impact differently. For some of you, leaning on close family and having emotional but needed conversations with your parents or carers may be the answer. It could be reaching out to friends and telling them how you feel, or even speaking to a professional. Whatever you need, your support system is valid and vital to recovering from this traumatic event.

If you are dealing with suicidal thoughts, or you've tried to take your own life, seek help. It's a well-worn message but help can show you a little light in the darkness. Please, remember that you are loved by many people in this world. You are cared for. You are an amazing human being with a wonderful future ahead of you. There are always more options than a single, final 'solution' and it might take just one conversation for you to realise that. Have that conversation. Fight your battle. Keep on surviving.

Resources

Websites

https://www.thetrevorproject.org/resources/preventing-suicide/ - information and resources on preventing suicide.
https://www.theproudtrust.org/for-young-people/advice-and-support/ - advice and support for LGBT+ people.
https://www.nhs.uk/oneyou/every-mind-matters - NHS youth mental health support.
https://www.papyrus-uk.org/help-advice/lgbtqia/ - suicide prevention advice for LGBTQIA+ people.
https://mindout.org.uk/ - LGBTQ mental health service.

Hotlines

0800 068 4141 – Papyrus, youth suicide prevention society.
0207 700 1323 – Pace Youth, free and confidential counselling for LGBTQ youth under 19.
116 123 – Samaritans, confidential support for people experiencing feelings of distress or despair.

Afterword

Hello again! Just finished reading the book? Or did you skip to the end to see what's here? Either way, welcome to the afterword! I had a couple more things I wanted to discuss here and it's a nice way to round things off, so let's get started.

As you can probably tell, the advice in each advice section is personal and straight from my heart. It's been researched thoroughly, but it's also me giving you some help which isn't a list of websites and phone numbers. It's what the youth workers who run BYOU would call 'lived experience'. I've been through life as an LGBT+ teen and, sometimes, a bit of reassurance from someone who's gone through the same thing you're going through is all you need.

On the following pages, you'll see a pretty extensive bibliography. This contains all the links I've used in researching this collection and can be used as 'further reading' if you so desire! It's basically a collection of all the resources combined with where I found the statistics which start each advice section.

One of the main reasons I have a bibliography is because this collection is being completed for my EPQ (Extended Project Qualification). I decided to write, publish and promote a collection of short stories for LGBT+ teens in the UK because it's a topic which is obviously close to my heart. So, in short, wish me luck!

With that, I'm going to end this book. Please, feel free to reread the stories as much as you want and check out the resources—they're there to help you! I hope you've enjoyed this collection!

-Oskar Leonard.

Bibliography

Albert Kennedy Trust (2015) *LGBT Youth Homelessness Report*. Available at: https://www.theproudtrust.org/wp-content/uploads/download-manager- files/AlbertKennedy_ResearchReport_Youth-Homelessness.pdf (Accessed: 2nd September 2020)

Albert Kennedy Trust (2020) *Home.* Available at: https://www.akt.org.uk/ (Accessed: 17th December 2020)

Ask The Police (2021) *Hate Crime/Incident Page*. Available at: https://www.askthe.police.uk /content/Q643.htm (Accessed: 2nd September 2020)

British Lung Foundation (2016) *Stoptober: the 28-day stop smoking challenge*. Available at: https://www.blf.org.uk/take-action/campaign-with-us/stoptober (Accessed: 3rd December 2020)

Childline (2021) *Home.* Available at: https://www.childline.org.uk/ (Accessed 2nd December 2020)

Consortium (2021) *Members Directory.* Available at: https://www.consortium.lgbt/member- directory (Accessed: 1st December 2020)

Counselling Directory (2021) *Gender dysphoria.* Available at: https://www.counselling-directory.org.uk/gender-identity.html (Accessed: 4th

December 2020)

GC2B (2020) *Safety Suggestions.* Available at:
https://gc2b.zendesk.com/hc/en-us/articles /
360036126234-Safety-Suggestions (Accessed: 2nd
September 2020)

Gendered Intelligence (2021) *Resources for Young
Trans People.* Available at: http://
genderedintelligence.co.uk/support/trans-youth/
resources (Accessed: 11th December 2020)

Gender Identity Development Service (2020)
Waiting Times Page. Available at: https://gic.nhs.uk/
appointments/waiting-times/ (Accessed: 2nd
September 2020)

Gender Identity Development Service (2020) *Home.*
Available at: https://gids.nhs.uk/ (Accessed: 4th
December 2020)

Government (2017) *National LGBT Survey Summary.*
Available at: https://www.gov.uk /government/
publications/national-lgbt-survey-summary-report/
national-lgbt-survey- summary-report#fn:18
(Accessed: 2nd September 2020)

Government (2021) *Marriages and civil partnerships
in England and Wales.* Available at: https://
www.gov.uk/marriages-civil-partnerships (Accessed:
8th December 2020)

Government (2021) *Help if you're homeless or about to become homeless.* Available at: https://www.gov.uk/if-youre-homeless-at-risk-of-homelessness (Accessed: 17th December)

Government (2021) *Your rights to housing if you're under 18.* Available at: https://www.gov.uk/your-rights-to-housing-if-youre-under-18 (Accessed: 17th December 2020)

Government (2021) *Change your name by deed poll.* Available at: https://www.gov.uk /change-name-deed-poll (Accessed: 20th December 2020)

Kooth (2021) *Home.* Available at: https://www.kooth.com (Accessed: 2nd December 2020)

Let's End Hate Crime (2020) *Home.* Available at: https://www.letsendhatecrime.com (Accessed: 2nd December 2020)

LGBT Foundation (2017) *How we can help you.* Available at: http://lgbt.foundation/how-we- can-help-you (Accessed: 5th December 2020)

Manchester Pride (2021) *Queer Black, BAME and POC Charities, Organisations and Community Groups.* Available at: https://www.manchesterpride.com/blog/queer- black-bame-and-poc-charities-organisations-and-community-groups (Accessed: 9th December 2020)

Mermaids (2021) *Home.* Available at: https://mermaidsuk.org.uk/ (Accessed: 4th December 2020)

Mind (2020) *LGBTIQ+ mental health.* Available at: https://www.mind.org.uk/information- support/tips-for-everyday-living/lgbtiqplus-mental-health/lgbtiqplus-mental-health- support/ (Accessed: 20th December 2020)

Mindout (2021) *Home.* Available at: https://mindout.org.uk/ (Accessed: 22nd December 2020)

National Health Service (2007) *A guide for young trans people in the UK.* Available at: https://www.east-ayrshire.gov.uk/Resources/PDF/L/LGBT-Guide-for-Young- Transgender-People.pdf (Accessed: 7th December 2020)

National Health Service (2018) *NHS stop smoking services help you quit.* Available at: https://www.nhs.uk/live-well/quit-smoking/nhs-stop-smoking-services-help-you-quit/ (Accessed: 3rd December 2020)

National Health Service (2018) *Under-18s guide to quitting smoking.* Available at: https://www.nhs.uk/live-well/quit-smoking/quitting-smoking-under-18s-guide/ (Accessed: 3rd December 2020)

National Health Service (2019) *Children and young people's mental health services (CYPMHS).* Available at: https://www.nhs.uk/using-the-nhs/nhs-services/mental- health-services/children-and-young-peoples-mental-health-services-cypmhs/ (Accessed: 21st December 2020)

National Health Service (2020) *Gender dysphoria.* Available at: https://www.nhs.uk /conditions/gender-dysphoria/ (Accessed: 2nd September 2020)

National Health Service (2020) *Every Mind Matters*. Available at: https://www.nhs.uk /oneyou/every-mind-matters (Accessed: 7th December 2020)

Northern Irish Government (2021) *Births, deaths, marriages and civil partnerships.* Available at: https://www.nidirect.gov.uk/information-and-services/government- citizens-and-rights/births-deaths-marriages-and-civil-partnerships (Accessed: 8th December 2020)

Office for National Statistics (2018) *Adult Smoking Habits In Great Britain.* Available at: https://www.ons.gov.uk/peoplepopulationandcommunity/healthandsocialcare /healthandlifeexpectancies/bulletins/adultsmokinghabitsingreatbritain /2019#characteristics-of-current-cigarette-smokers-in-the-uk (Accessed: 2nd September 2020)

Papyrus (2021) *LGBTQIA+.* Available at: https://www.papyrus-uk.org/help-advice/lgbtqia/ (Accessed: 22nd December 2020)

Prince's Trust (2020) *LGBT+ Resources.* Available at: https://www.princes-trust.org.uk/help- for-young-people/who-else/housing-health-wellbeing/wellbeing/sexuality (Accessed: 20th December 2020)

Say It (2020) *LGBT+ Faith and BAMER support groups.* Available at: https://sayit.org.uk /wp-content/uploads/2020/01/LGBT-Faith-and-BAMER-support-groups-1.pdf (Accessed: 15th December 2020)

Scottish Government (2021) *Marriages and civil partnerships.* Available at: https://www.mygov.scot/births-deaths-marriages/marriage-civil-partnerships/ (Accessed: 8th December 2020)

Shelter (2020) *Help if you're homeless: 16 and 17 year olds.* Available at: https://england.shelter.org.uk/housing_advice/homelessness /help_if_youre_homeless_16_and_17_year_olds (Accessed: 17th December 2020)

Stonewall (2016) *LGBT Facts And Figures.* Available at: https://www.stonewall.org.uk /media/lgbt-facts-and-figures (Accessed: 2nd September 2020)

Stonewall (2017) *The School Report.* Available at: https://www.stonewall.org.uk/system/files /the_school_report_2017.pdf (Accessed: 2nd September 2020)

Stonewall (2017) *BAME and POC LGBT Communities.* Available at: https://www.stonewall.org.uk/bame-and-poc-lgbt-communities (Accessed: 9th December 2020)

Stonewall (2017) *Conversion Therapy.* Available at: https://www.stonewall.org.uk/campaign-groups/conversion-therapy (Accessed: 19th December 2020)

Stonewall (2018) *LGBT Britain Health.* Available at: https://www.stonewall.org.uk/lgbt- britain-health (Accessed: 2nd September 2020)

Stonewall (2020) *Resources for LGBT People Of Faith.* Available at: https://www.stonewall.org.uk/resources-lgbt-people-faith (Accessed: 15th December 2020)

Stonewall Scotland (2019) *QTIPOC organisations you should know about.* Available at: https://www.stonewallscotland.org.uk/about-us/news/qtipoc-organisations-you- should-know-about (Accessed: 9th December 2020)

Stop Hate UK (2020) *Report LGBTQI+ Hate Crime.* Available at: https://www.stophateuk.org/report-lgb-and-t-hate-crime/ (Accessed: 16th December 2020)

Stop Smoking (2020) *Local help and support.* Available at: https://www.stopsmokingni.info /ways-quit/local-help-and-support (Accessed: 3rd

December 2020)

The Proud Trust (2020) *Advice And Support*. Available at: https://www.theproudtrust.org/for-young-people/advice-and-support/ (Accessed: 14th December 2020)

The Trevor Project (2021) *Preventing Suicide*. Available at: https://www.thetrevorproject.org /resources/preventing-suicide/ (Accessed: 22nd December 2020)

Trevor Space (2020) *Home*. Available at: https://www.trevorspace.org (Accessed: 1st December 2020)

Young Minds (2021) *Find help*. Available at: https://youngminds.org.uk/find-help/ (Accessed: 7th December 2020)

Lightning Source UK Ltd.
Milton Keynes UK
UKHW020638190321
380637UK00011B/565